Village Stories
2021

**An Anthology with Articles from
25 Laguna Woods Publishing Club Authors**

By

Peggy P. Edwards

Other Publishing Club publications:

Village Stories 2015
Village Stories 2016
Village Stories 2017
Village Stories 2018
Village Stories 2019
Village Stories 2020

Introduction

Flowers, Flowers Everywhere
Fred Cantor

Looking Over the Fence
Nancy Brown

Table of Contents

Six Years of Stirring Stories
Peggy P. Edwards

Foreword
Peggy P. Edwards

This is our seventh edition of "Village Stories." We have published an anthology once a year since 2015. This year's 25 authors wrote stories, poems, songs, and essays. Memoirs are a favorite, but we also write fiction.

Sunshine, our publisher, memoirist, and even song guru, Dennis Glauber, our Shakespearian classicist, Lorraine Gow, our magical realist, Phil Silverman, our Village entertainer delving in theater as well as poetry, Ellyn Maybe, our famous poet, Jon

Perkins, our *noir* storyteller – have all been with us since the beginning.

Jerry Schur weaves his stories with a thread of humor, while Jack Mullen and Alan Dale Dickinson create very human heroes. Scott Galasso is our master poet. Daneen Pysz highlights women in the Bible. Peg Zuber illustrates her Biblical points. Daya Shankar teaches us Indian history as S. Ramagopal exemplifies it. Barbara Ashley shows us how to write a good book. Cheryl Silverman garnishes it with haiku.

Philosophical memoirs are authored by Barbara De Marco Barrett, Nancy Brown, Beth Cornelius, Denise Conner and Carol Kangas. Doug Sainsbury observes with nostalgia. Marcia Hackett's is a universal frustration with SPAM. Fred Cantor is a sports enthusiast while my path led me to other famous personages.

We hope to live by our philosophies and our stories. We publish not only for our reading pleasure but also for posterity – for future generations of Village dwellers who then will weave their stories into ours.

Four Paths or more to a story
Peggy P. Edwards

Some Things are Just Meant to Be
Carol Kangas

I was a divorced woman, raising my two children from a previous marriage, living with my mother and working full time. I was also in my 40's. After attending the wedding of my best friend's daughter, I was introduced to a man whose wife had recently died, after a 35-year marriage. We had both attended the same high school and his wife was my best friend's cousin. Small world.

After this first encounter, we began seeing each other. The one snag in this friendship was that he lived 120 miles from where I lived. He had retired after his wife's passing, and I was working full-time and quite happy with my life's situation. After commuting and dating for three years, I was given the decision to marry or not. This was a big decision, as I wasn't comfortable with quitting my job, with its great benefits and 401K plan, moving from the home my mother and I had purchased and entering into the unknown. My faith played a big part in my decision. We were married, rented his home, and moved into mine.

At the time, my mother was in failing health; however, with him being home with her most of the time, my kids continuing school and my job being three miles from home, we had a good arrangement. Since he had retired from being a carpenter, his hobby was to refurbish the house. It went from a little tract home to a customized, beautiful little piece of paradise. He added a garden room, built a deck and gazebo around our above-ground pool, built a treehouse for the kids, a shed for our garden tools and converted the garage into a workshop. We planted a couple of fruit trees and had a beautiful assortment of rose bushes.

Someone I met at a dinner party asked, "How old were you when you married?" When I said 45, he said, "Wow, that's like finding a needle in a haystack!"

My lucky haystack. We enjoyed 29 years together. He had never flown on a plane until after we married. And we were lucky enough to travel abroad while we could still walk miles at a time and enjoy the sights, friends and adventures of life.

After suffering from dementia and Alzheimer's for quite some time, he declined in health quickly. My husband will be my hero forever.

Matters of Grave Concern
Dennis Glauber

I have never been particularly attracted to, or especially repelled by cemeteries and graveyards. On my travels I have visited the great and famous in places like Highgate in London and Pere Lachaise in Paris. And I have been to the graveyard of Trinity Church in Stratford-on-Avon to pay obeisance to you know who.

But a new dimension has been added to my experience. In the early years of this century, I was exposed to the intellectual and emotional experience of visiting some of the World War I graves in Flanders and in France. We made annual visits to Brussels where our son David and his family had been living since 2000, and I became infected with David's enthusiasm and some of his immense knowledge of that conflict.

It was with eager anticipation that he and I set out one weekend in 2002 to visit some of the cemeteries in Flanders and then to the Somme region of Picardy in France. Our first stop was no more than an hour's drive from Brussels, the cemetery of St. Symphorien, a place of pastoral serenity. The grounds are on several levels laid out with rockeries and flower beds like an English country garden. In every direction there was something poignant to observe...the grave of the first Englishman to die in August 1914 and not far from that of the last Englishman killed on November 11, 1918. And as though to trump that agonizing misfortune, I saw and photographed the grave of a Canadian soldier killed at 10:58 a.m. on that day (1918), just two minutes before the end of hostilities.

Among the allied gravestones was a sprinkling of German graves. And among the endless array of crosses were several Stars of David. It was there that we learned that when the Germans again occupied Belgium during World War II, the SS set out to destroy the graves of Jewish German troops of World War I.

Colonel (later Field Marshal) von Mannstein defied Himmler's orders and posted troops to protect the graves of Jewish Germans who had died for their fatherland a quarter century earlier.

In the Somme one is overwhelmed by the sheer scale of the carnage. The dead are numbered not in the hundreds of thousands but in the millions. There are hundreds of graveyards of varying sizes. On just the first day of the Second Battle of the Somme in

July 1916 over 20,000 British troops were killed! I could describe Beaumont Hamel where the entire Newfoundland Regiment was annihilated and where there are still restrictions of movement because of the possible presence of live shells. I could write about Delville Wood where 4000 South Africans entered the forest to root out the Germans, and on the sixth day only 129 survivors emerged. I could describe Thiepval where a huge (and hideous) memorial bears the names of over 73,000 soldiers who have no known remains or burial place.

Graves containing the remains of individuals uniformly bear only the name and regiment of the deceased, and all too many of them, for lack of identification, bear the words coined by Rudyard Kipling, "a soldier known but to God."

The scale is so enormous that one attempts to personalize the experience for the sake of perspective. Such an opportunity presented itself on a visit we made in 2003 to the largest Military Cemetery in Britain, Brookwood not far from London. There on a memorial bearing the names of 3500 men and women of the forces "to whom the fortune of war denied a known and honoured grave", David spotted one K E Glauber, a sergeant in the Royal Regiment of Artillery. We began our research. We learned that he was Kurt Erich Glauber, born in Vienna and a resident of Paddington in London where he lived with his parents. He was born in1902 and had a law doctorate from the University of Vienna. He was clearly part of an Austrian Jewish family that had managed to find an English refuge from Nazi Europe. But we were intrigued. Why would a 42-year-old lawyer be serving as a sergeant in the artillery, and how did he die? David's research continued and yielded this fascinating story.

Daniza Ilitsch (born in Belgrade as Danica Ilic) was a famous soprano at the Vienna State Opera from 1936 until 1951. She also sang many roles at the Metropolitan Opera in New York in two seasons immediately after World War II. She was close to the anti-Nazi underground in Vienna, which almost cost her, her life. She and her sister hid a British agent working for the secret service M I6 in their apartment for nearly six months. When the agent was finally arrested in January 1945, the sisters were taken into custody and survived in a camp until Vienna was liberated by the Red Army in April 1945. The agent was not so fortunate and was murdered in Mauthausen Concentration camp in April. He was, of course, Kurt Erich Glauber. His story is rounded off a year later with a War Office announcement on June 6, 1946, of a posthumous King's commendation for brave conduct.

Our quest for a personal connection based on our fairly uncommon surname was successful, and I only wish I knew what our namesake's spying mission was. In any event, I hope I never become too blasé and too jaded to lose that sense of shock and awe. God forbid that one should ever be unaffected by the horror that is war, any war.

Sobriety
Denise Conner

On May 1, 2021, I celebrated seven years of sobriety. I never thought I'd be able to do it. I loved the taste of red wine, and the intoxicating feelings too much. I didn't feel the need to drink every day; most of the time I could stop drinking after just one...or maybe two glasses.

But there would always be that one night where I didn't want to stop—where I truly felt like I couldn't stop, and where I just kept on drinking. I'd throw away all my inhibitions and be the life of the party. I'd of course feel like hell the next day, swear off drinking for a month or two, or even six, and then the drinking of one glass or two at night would creep back in. I would wonder to myself...how in the world will I ever be able to stop?

Throughout my life, ever since I'd had my first drink, the one-night-can't-stop-til-I'm-too-drunk-to-walk experience, would occur occasionally – maybe only once a year or every other year. When I was out drinking with friends, I allowed it to happen more often, and it was even more dangerous for me. If I did it when I was home alone, the only bad thing that ever happened was waking up the next day feeling very sick.

There were some truly horrible events in my life that occurred only because I drank too much. My first experience happened with my very first drink. I was 17 with coworkers at a bowling alley; they bought me the first drinks. I loved the taste and feeling so much that I got beyond tipsy and had my one-and-only extremely terrifying DUI experience. Luckily, I made it home safe and sound with no one and nothing hurt, stayed under the radar, and learned the "never-drink-and-drive lesson."

Another time, I almost lost my life. I was in the Army in Germany; somehow got so drunk that I fell three and a half floors, straight down, landing on the concrete basement floor. But apparently that lesson wasn't enough. It wasn't until I lost something truly precious to me -- a career goal, a once-in-a-lifetime achievement, that I finally learned. I was sent home in disgrace and shame. When I looked longingly at the airport bar, it beckoned me with the temptation to drown my sorrows. I knew it couldn't surpass the grief in my heart for that lost dream. I decided that day, from that moment forward, I would choose to be sober. I would choose for me.

For a while I had to choose every single moment. But when temptation beckoned, I would remember the feeling I had on that flight home. I knew deep inside me that if I took even one drink, it would be throwing away my final lesson; all the pain, suffering and grief would have been for naught.

It was this second fall, the fall from grace that truly saved my life.

I knew deep inside that if I could survive the death of my dream, it meant I was strong. More than that, it meant that I truly had within me the inner strength to stop drinking all along. I just had to recognize that strength and claim it as my own. I also went out and got help through attending AA meetings.

With strength and help from my friends, I rose from the ashes, gathered my courage, listened to the universe, and was rewarded with the most wondrous life gifts of all.

I want you to know if you're struggling, if you fall, that even if you have trouble seeing it, you really do have the strength inside you to rise again.

The Walker
Doug Sainsbury

Two years ago in January, I noted a man walking in front of my condo in Laguna Woods Village. He was dressed in a hoodie/windbreaker, long nylon gym pants, a baseball type cap with the hoodie pulled over the top, and he wore sunglasses. The only visible parts of his face were his dark cheeks and chin. His route took him past my condo on the grass next to the golf cart path on a par five hole. Apparently, he preferred this outdoor exercise to the confines of one of the gyms in the village.

He walked several hundred yards to the green on the par five hole, turned, and walked back in front of my condo to a driveway leading to a parking lot. However, before entering the parking lot, he spun and retraced his steps back onto the lawn in front of my condo. I watched as this man headed for his second lap on the course that he had walked a few minutes prior. After several of these round trips, he continued walking toward the parking lot and did not return.

I speculated regarding the purpose of his routine. Former military man? A workout regimen to lose weight? He appeared to be somewhat overweight. He was probably five foot eight or nine inches tall and could have been in his 50s, 60s, or 70s.

This walker initiated his routine daily, usually between noon and three o'clock. Once or twice each week, he would pause in the middle of his routine and lie on his back on the grass in front of my condo and stretch, perform push-ups, and other exercises. I have never seen him standing in conversation with any other residents of the village. He would wave to others as they passed.

As the days, weeks, and months passed, the walker did not vary his routine. Occasionally his attire would change, but he was always covered from head to toe. Winter morphed into spring, then summer arrived, and I wondered if I would see him, and if so, would he still be bundled up? Yes, on both counts. I could only speculate as to how his "uniform" must generate rivers of sweat, and the discomfort he was experiencing.

During the early days of the pandemic, I did not see the walker execute his routine as some heavy rain made for sloppy conditions on the grass. Did he have COVID? Was he ill from some other malady? As the heavy rains subsided, I saw the walker return to his routine, but now he was wearing a mask. Light rain did not stop him.

Spring and summer crept in as they always do, surprising us with the stealth of their emergence. I noticed that the walker seemed different somehow. Was he walking faster? No, he was thinner. His regimen had enabled him to shed some pounds; or was this unintentional?

As 2020 rumbled on, the walker's jacket began to hang on his once-burly frame. Now in 2021, he was remarkably thinner. He must have lost fifty pounds. Yet, still, he walks. I wonder when or if he will ever attain his goal.

Forest Gumpess
Peggy P. Edwards

I was born to flitter around center stage in two countries.

At a mere seven years, I danced solo with a partner at the iconic performing arts center, Palacio de Bellas Artes in Mexico City for Presidente Miguel Alemán.

My great uncle, Tom Miller, established the first General Motors dealership in Mexico City. He purchased the conqueror, Pedro Alvarado's home in Coyoacan, Mexico and threw many a party there. We, of course, were always invited. Among his guests were Frida Kahlo and Diego Rivera. Dolores del

Rio was his neighbor and Trotsky was murdered down the block. He gave refuge to King Carol of Romania who became my sister's Godfather.

He also owned a cliff-side mansion in Acapulco where John Wayne hung out because my uncle's cook, Margarita, was renowned for her culinary delights which included the tequila 'Margarita.'

My paternal grandmother, Frances Miller Parmelee's odyssey from San Antonio, Texas to Los Angeles, California took place in 1923, and was recorded and photographed for perpetuity. At about the same time, my maternal grandfather, Merrell Russey, was working in the Mexican silver mines while taking correspondence courses from Thomas Alba Edison. This knowledge enabled him to transform the world's largest silver mines from mule driven to electricity driven, thus saving hundreds of lives and cruelty to the mules.

My maternal grandmother's family migrated to Mexico from Cornwall, England to help work the silver mines. Her brother, Alfred Crowle, organized the first successful soccer team in Mexico and thus, was considered a national hero.

President Richard Nixon visited our bilingual elementary school in Mexico City and greeted us during our PE class.

During my sophomore high school year, I fell in love with Carlos Turpin. His best friend, Artemio Portes Gil, was the son of Mexico's president, Artemio Portes Gil. He dated my sister, and a composer wrote "Maria Elena," dedicated to his wife. My sister's name is Marilyn and so she assumed it was written in her honor.

Carlos was the captain of his school's soccer team and, as such, invited me to ride in his school parade as a princess. Flor Silvestre, a very famous Mexican chanteuse, accompanied me and was the queen. My father sold her a green and silver Buick which was later our car.

Jerry Lee Lewis performed at our high school my junior year. I invited him to a party at my home in the Lomas de Chapultepec that same evening. He came with his band and played his rocking tunes on our master piano.

President John Kennedy and his wife Jackie attended our high school 4th of July celebration in 1962, my senior year. I, as part of our school parade, was able to shake their hands. Jackie was especially admired because she spoke Spanish as well as English.

One of my best friends and neighbors was Virginia Sendel, a well-known celebrity in Mexico who established "Michou y Mau," a burn victim sanctuary. She also wrote "México Mágico" relating the magic of Mexico's pyramids and other treasures.

Virginia's mother was Rebeca Iturbide, one of Mexico's first TV actresses, but she was best known as "Miss Pepsi Cola" which she represented on TV and even used on her hair instead of hair spray.

I traveled with Ginny (Virginia Sendel) and her mother Rebeca, to Acapulco. We dined at La Perla, the famous cliff-diving location where we were introduced to Debby Reynolds and Eddie Fisher.

In 1962, I enrolled at Southern Methodist University in Dallas, Texas. Sadly, the following year there, President Kennedy was murdered in Dallas. My son claims he still suspects me. ☺

A Dallas boyfriend invited me to water ski and on our way to Lake Dallas, he picked up Warren Beatty. While flitting along on his speed boat, Warren Beatty stood up and fell on top of me. He sang, "Getting to Know You" as he struggled to remove himself from my lap.

I was a stewardess for the famous Troy Post, Braniff Airlines. We flew the colored Calder planes and wore the Pucci outfits while we performed the airline strip.

While working on my Masters' degree at the University of Wisconsin, I met the great basketball star, Karim Abdul Jabar, at my neighbor's party.

Years later, while working with Michelle Phillips' sister at Catholic Charities during Amnesty, I met Michelle of the 'Mamas and Papas."

Due to an attempted overthrow at American Immigrant Foundation, for which I was CEO, I made an appointment with the famous feminist lawyer, Gloria Allred. She came out to meet me, looked me over once, did an about face and returned to her office. Her secretary said, "Ms. Allred will not take your case." When I returned to my car hang-faced, I realized I was wearing my red St. John Knit suit inside out.

I was asked to teach dual immersion (English and Spanish) at a newly established preschool, El Sol Elementary in Santa Ana. The school was funded by Paul Merage, a billionaire and the creator of "Hot Pockets."

He also funded the School of Business at U.C. Irvine. He invited us to his home in Newport Beach, a mansion resembling a museum of fine art.

My brother-in-law, Air Force Col. Frank Thieme, was buried in Arlington Memorial Cemetery, a victim of Agent Orange.

This year, 2021, I edited the book of Elmer Armstrong of the last Platters band. He has invited me to dinner next week.

My son is the Air Force, Space Force Deputy Commander.

I played ukulele with the famous ukulele master, Bill Tapia.

The most effective influence in my life was my husband, Ron. We celebrated forty years of marriage. He passed away July 15. He was born in Chitenango, New York, the birthplace of L. Frank Baum, author of the "Wizard of Oz." My birth name is Dorothy and Ron piloted a hot-air balloon. One day in May, he left New York behind in search of his Dorothy, and so we lived happily ever after.

We are our stories and mine has been part of many other stories – the famous and not-so-famous, but nonetheless, fascinating.

Who knows who I will meet next? But meanwhile, I'm happy compiling our *Village Stories*, because together we weave our stories.

A Bit of Christmas
From the Gifts' Point of View
Sunshine Lutey

I was sleeping peacefully when I was rudely awakened by a sudden bright light. I felt hands that extracted me from a dark interior and set me down upon a kitchen counter. I heard a sudden exclamation in a high voice, "Oh my!"

I watched a woman opening packages. She was grinning broadly. She seemed to be in a hurry and, as she turned a bit wildly, she knocked something off the counter onto the floor. It made a loud crash.

A voice called, "Sunshine, are you all right?"

"I'm okay, David; I just dropped something; it wasn't breakable . . . just wait til I show you what Denise sent to us!"

I'm a 12-ounce unbreakable cup with a lid that closes tightly; my lid has a slide which can be opened for drinking. I remember nothing before being awakened; perhaps Sunshine brought me to life. I like how I look with silver trim and decorations all over my body. I think I'll call myself 'Handy.'"

There were two more cups; one had a design that was similar to mine but had no

 handle. The other cup resembled a thermos. I think it keeps drinks hot or cold.

I nodded at them, but they didn't respond; maybe they weren't awake yet. "Are you awake?"

"Good grief! Who could sleep through that; I'm awake! I'm a proud 'YETI Rambler' cup!"

"Well, I'm awake, too. I am 'Silver' and I'm proud of my silvery sheen!"

"Hey, I'm 'Holder'; you didn't even look at me! Have you ever seen a more gorgeous tote bag?

Sunshine carried us to another room  where a man was sitting on the couch. We heard her say, "Look David! It really is Christmas! Denise sent these cups and a beautiful musical tote bag for me. She sent something for you, too. I think you will like your present."

Handy remarked, "I don't think David can see very well as David asked, 'What is it?'"

Sunshine leaned closer and explained, "Look; it's a five-pound bag of orange slices, and another bag over three pounds. You

 won't run out of orange slices for a long time! Here, try one. I put some of the candy in a container for you. I had one and it was delicious."

By this time 'Candy' was awake, "You better believe he'll like us; we're the best!"

David tried one of the orange slices, "These orange slices are really good! What are you going to do with all those cups, Sunshine?"

Handy could see Sunshine's furrowed brow as she considered. With a smile she announced, "Well, I know exactly what I'm going to do – they are all unbreakable and they have covers. I can drink from them without using a straw, so I don't get bubbles when I drink. If I accidentally tip them over, they won't spill. You know, I really like them. I will keep the big dark gray one for when I drive in my car because it keeps drinks either hot or cold."

Yeti snobbishly replied, "Just as it should be! YETIs are VIP and like to travel!"

Sunshine continued, "The silver one with the musical decorations will stay on my nightstand. I'll use it at night when I need water."

Silver spoke with pride, "Ah! I have the best job! I'll watch over her as she sleeps and give her water when her mouth feels dry."

Finally, Sunshine looked at me. "The cup with the musical decorations and the handle, I'll use it when I sit here in the living room with you, David. I'll have it with me when I eat my dinner, and while I watch a movie with you. I like all the cups, but I think I like the one with the handle best."

I smiled to myself and announced to everyone, "How do you think this makes me feel? I really like this place."

I'm not sure Sunshine or David heard me, but I heard a collective sigh from Candy, Holder, Silver, and even Yeti. "Oh yes! So nice!"

Childhood Run
Phil Silverman

Childhood, a precious thing
Goes away but stays until the early spring
The summer brings forth the rush of youth
For 48-year-old dudes
At a folk festival in Mantaloking

Folk is okay and light jazz is nice
Sausages and fruit drinks,
funnel cakes are fine
Speeches and announcements
permeate the air
For 48-year-old dudes
Walking with a mixed drink
and with great care

Maybe she'll show up; she loves folk jazz
She did say she might make it
if she's got some gas
The sun at 95 brings out much fashion
For 49-year-old ladies
Still denying their passion

Yeah, she never showed up
So, I sat by rusted go-carts
with my empty cup
Now it's 4:45pm and I'm ready to drive
See Monday ahead and so an early bed

Credit card bills to arrive.
So, it's off to that parking lot, walkin' alone
Steppin' across those
coal-colored pointy stones
I'm tired but feel an insistent spark
Something from childhood life
musta left its mark
Dad, I'm gonna run like Mantle!

Fear and Greed
Jon Perkins

Heavyset and sweating, Theo brushed drops of dew from his black brows. He looked across the table at the Asian with thick puce lips and close-set eyes partially hidden by an exceptionally large epicanthic fold. Zhang Min's face was impassive as usual. His hands were calm, folded together in his lap. His biceps stretched the fabric of a colorful silk Kimono aloha shirt.

"There is no forgiveness," Min said. "The choice was yours, not ours."

"I didn't know."

Min's head dropped back, and his maw of a mouth opened wide to sputter a high-pitched laugh. "Hahaha." Filaments of spit sprayed the elegant Persian carpet. "So you confess? You try to undo what has been done?"

"The picture then wasn't clear."

"Second thoughts? Second thoughts bad. Death sentence."

A shudder wormed through Theo's fat frame. "You wouldn't!"

Min stood. He took a second to observe the man sitting on the opulent sofa with a mouth expressing just the barest hint of contempt. "Goodbye, Mister Theo. I let myself out."

Theo bent over, elbows on knees, hands cradling his head, Theo reflected on his long-lasting association with the inscrutable Zhang Min. The day he was first approached, eating a tuna sandwich in the lunchroom at Telemere Tech, he was surprised and not a little bit offended by the stranger who sat down next to him at the otherwise empty table.

"You not important man." The words spoken by the person who appeared from nowhere angered Theo. His hand grabbed the sandwich and was about to be thrust back into the Kraft bag when the man spoke again. "Wait. No trouble. Good news for you."

"Well, what do you want? I've never seen you before. Do you work here?"

"You be rich, important man."

"What?"

"The genetic code. Simple thing. I would like to have it."

"What?" Theo repeated. He squinted his eyes. "Who do you work for? Why on earth would I give you our secrets? I'm not a spy!"

"Just for me. I die of dreadful disease, need to make cure."

Theo leaned back in his chair. "We're not a pharmaceutical company, whoever you are."

"No, no. Not medication. My name Zhang Min. I die of genetic disease unless find cure."

"That's just pie in the sky, Mister Zhang. We've only just begun to understand the function of the strand we're working on."

"Min. My name Min."

"Min, you ask too much. I cannot give you the code. I'm sorry."

"I rich man. Much money. I share with you for code."

Theo thought about this strange person with his strange request. "You would share the code with others?"

"No share! Just me!"

Theo thought some more, risk versus reward. His eyes bored into those of the other person. "How much?"

A smile drew the corners of Min's mouth outward. He knew at that moment he'd get what he came for.

"Much! I die, no use for money. I find cure, better than money!"

Theo waited. A hand on the table began to play a piano tune, fingers thumping to unheard music.

"One million dollars."

The hand ceased playing. Theo's face betrayed the thoughts coalescing in his brain.

"Today. Right now. I get code, you get money."

"I don't know, Min. Sounds too good to be true."

"I not only one you give data to."

"What?"

"Mister Ellis. You give data to Mister Ellis."

"How do you know that!" Theo sat forward; his shoulders hunched in a crouch.

"Telemere not happy they find out."

Theo stood. He began to pace under Min's watchful eyes.

"No problem, Mister Theo. Just for me. So I live."

Theo stood, his eyes unseeing, weighing the pluses and the minuses. Eventually, he reached the only conclusion he could.

"Fear and greed," he said.

"What?" Min asked.

"Fear and greed. It's always been like that. From day one."

"What mean?"

"Okay, Min. I'm in. I give you the code, you give me the million dollars."

Min's grin widened. "Shake?"

"No shake. You'll get what you came for."

Theo, sitting on the sofa after Min had departed, dropped his hands from his face and searched the ceiling with his eyes. He wanted desperately to forget, to have his brain as blank as the stucco ceiling. A low moan escaped his lips.

"Fear and greed. That's why people fail. Why nations fail."

Everything I Need to Know I Learned
From 12 Bible Stories
Peg Zuber

1. to *forgive* others
   Joseph & his brothers

2. to *run from temptation*
   ...Joseph & Potiphar's wife

3. to have *victory*
   Joshua & Jericho

4. to *depend* on God
   David & Goliath

5. to be a *friend*
   David & Jonathan

6. to *defend* my faith
   Esther & Mordecai

7. to seek God's
      protection
   Shadrach, Meshach,
      & Abednego

8. to *trust* God
   Daniel & the Lion's Den

9. to honor my mother
   & father
   Ruth & Naomi

10. to not be *anxious,*
    Jesus Sermon
    on the Mount

11. to know God's
    abundance
    Jesus feeds the
    five thousand

12. to have *faith,*
    not *doubt*
    Peter walks on
    water

Charlie, the Private Eye in Syria
Alan Dale Dickinson

No, my friends, Charles Warner Kennedy "Charlie" O'Brien, the world renowned, and quite successful Private Investigator, is not dead; he is actually very much alive.

He was located by Jan Smoker, Director of the Agency (The Central Intelligence Agency) from Langley, Virginia. She is a good friend of Charlie's and they have solved many crimes together.

To the many people who attended his celebrated and heart-wrenching home going (funeral) at the Arlington National Cemetery, they will all be totally shocked to hear the great news. Charlie's back!

It turned out to be an empty coffin that they buried at the Cemetery, which was a way for Charlie to leave the country for the Middle East, without any notice by anyone.

He was located in Syria in the quite dangerous and very volatile northern part of the war-torn country. President Bashar Assad, with assistance from the Russian army/navy, (and President Vladimir Putin), are fighting the Northern Alliance.

FSA [Free Syrian Army] was formed on July 29, 2011.

This Alliance is made up of a variety of different nationalities including Kurds, Turks, Iraqis, Syrian freedom fighters, several defectors from Assad's Army, Sunni Muslims, Druze, Christians from Northern Iraq, and also some Palestinians.

Charlie and Sundee, were quite surprised, when they arrived to see how well all of these different groups got along, and fought side-by-side, without any difficulties at all.

Charlie has some relatives who were fighting with the FSA Alliance; they convinced him to come and give them some advice on their efforts to Free Syria from President Assad.

Our man Charlie was mostly Irish, a little bit English and also part Iraqi. He speaks a little of the Syrian language, and Farci, just enough to get by, if necessary.

Charlie took with him *Sundee Marie Law*, his favorite and long-time sidekick, *Sarge*, (J. J. *Hernandez*), a retired OCSD [Orange County Sheriff Department] sergeant, and *Peggy Edwards*, who is a communication, and foreign language expert.

Charlie did not take his entire A-Team on this trip as he felt that it would be just too dangerous for them; therefore, he selected just his best three associates to watch his back.

Charlie felt that this could quite easily be a 'Death Mission,' and Sundee, Sarge, and Peggy all volunteered immediately as soon as he asked them.

He was thrilled that he had them along for his dangerous trek and was extremely glad that he did not have to go alone as he had expected.

Sundee is very sharp, quick to action, strong and very fit, as well as very intelligent. She is an expert in Middle East culture and speaks Farci and several other dialects.

Sarge is the bravest and toughest man Charlie has ever known; he truly is an expert at hand-to-hand combat, explosives and all types of weapons.

Peggy is a communication and foreign language expert; she also speaks several different languages. Her husband Ron is a retired New York Police Watch Commander.

Ron really wanted to come with Charlie; however, he had to stay home and take care of their two very active cats--Chula and Bootsy. One just loves to get out of the house and climb up on the roof, and then cannot get down!

Success! The four of them, what Charlie called his C-Team, were able, with the needed assistance of the FSA 'freedom fighters,' to free the oppressed and tormented people in three Northern Syria towns.

In a heartbeat, they were on a jet-plane back to Los Angeles, California, the City of the Angels. Charlie always likes to tell people; "I love that dirty air; L.A. you're my town."

How You Can Tell Your Own Great Stories
Barbara Ashley

What is a Story?

"Our lives are stories, not plots." Author unknown

"A unified action that creates a whole made up of a beginning, a middle, and an end." Aristotle

"What is truer than truth? A story – in a story we distill data and give it meaning." David Hoffman

"The first condition of Art is that it contains nothing that is not essential." Andre Gide

A story is also a metaphor, a model of some aspect of human behavior. It is a thought machine by which we explore our ideas and feelings about some human quality and try to learn more about it." Christopher Vogler

What Makes Your Story a Great Story?

1) A **Great Story** poses or answers important questions and/or inspires your audience to ask or answer such questions.

   What would I have done in a similar challenging situation?

2) **Great Stories** are based upon or inspired by a fundamental and significant theme, premise or moral. If you want to tell an authentic and entertaining story, your theme must be one that aligns with your personal values/morals.

3) **Great Stories** satisfy universal emotional needs, fears and aspirations. We all want/need to love and be loved, to be appreciated for our unique and true selves, to find satisfaction in our work, to feel safe and secure and to express ourselves creatively.

4) A **Great Story** is told and executed in such a way that captures and sustains the interest of your audience.

5) Versions and adaptations of some **Great Stories** have been told and retold for thousands of years. Many of these stories evolved from myths and legends.

6) **Great Stories** appeal to a broad audience of both sexes, different ages, cultures and educational backgrounds.

7) **Great Stories** explore broad cultural elements and trends: human rights, religious beliefs, role of technology, etc.

8) Many **Great Stories** have been adapted into a wide variety of media and formats (books, screen and stage plays, etc.)

9) A **Great Story** needs a great title because it is usually the first and may be the only thing your potential audience sees – your only chance to capture their attention. The most important goal of your title is to make your potential audience want to experience your story. Titles of a single or very few words are often the most effective and memorable. (*Jaws, Titanic*)

Great titles often include intriguing words or phrases and may include "Emotional Triggers" such as death, life, terror, heaven, hell, the sun, planets and moons, rage, mystery, hidden, devil, God, etc.

Sources of Great Titles, Themes, Characters & Names

1) **Mythology** – Supernatural Beings like gods, goddesses, angels, demons, ghosts, fairies, Places like Valhalla, Hades

2) **Legends** – Paul Bunyan

3) **Poetry** – *Paradise Lost, Song of Hiawatha* (Robert Blake)

4) **Religious, Spiritual and Philosophical Works** - the *Bible*, the *Koran*, *The Power of Myth* (Joseph Campbell)

5) **Proverbs, Folklore, Aphorisms** – "Birds of a feather flock together." "All's well that ends well."

6) **Clichés or Wordplay on clichéd words or phrases**

7) **Classical Literature and Other Arts**

8) **Sciences** – Significant Discoveries and Innovations

9) **Historical Events and Characters** – Wars, Immigration and Emigration, Rise and Fall of Empires and Governments

Great Stories Need Great Characters

Great Characters are unique, charismatic, often larger than life humans or other **Sentient Beings (**can think, feel, act and react) who have compelling and fundamental needs, desires and goals, who are driven to take action to get what they need or want. A **Great Character** is a credible and interesting blend of strengths, weaknesses, virtues and flaws, much like us and almost everyone we've ever known.

1) **Protagonist(s) -** Your main character or characters – the person(s), animals, extraterrestrials or other sentient beings your story is about. This character or characters must have a goal/ quest or a challenge they must overcome.

2) **Antagonist** – Character, Entity or Force that challenges, opposes or resists the Protagonist, blocking/preventing him/her/them from accomplishing their goal(s)

Iconic Characters appear repeatedly in **Great Stories** in every time, place and culture. Examples: Lovers, Rulers, Healers, Warriors, Shamans/Priestesses/Clergy,

Criminals, Artists, Educators, Adventurers/Explorers, etc.

Archetypes are flexible character functions or roles rather than rigid character types. In any given story, any character may play more than one function or role.

Archetypes are "Constantly recurring characters who appear in the dreams of all peoples and the myths of all cultures." (Jung)

> **Hero/Heroine/Antihero** – Essence is self-sacrifice on behalf of a group, an individual or an ideal (freedom, equality, etc.) and the search for identity, balance and wholeness.
>
> **Friends, Allies, Supporters** – Characters who support, accompany and share the struggles, accomplishments and setbacks of the Protagonist or Antagonist
>
> **Parents, Nurturers** – Characters who give birth, raise and/or provide food, clothing and shelter to other characters in need
>
> **Teachers, Mentors** – Characters who represent the higher self/conscience of hero/heroine, who advise, teach, guide,

test or train others – may be a book, image, map, a dream or vision etc. rather than a sentient being

Shapeshifters – Primary characteristic is that they appear to change from the hero/heroine's point of view (behavior, speech, disguises, masks, etc.). Often, they are of the opposite sex of the hero/heroine, of another species or a supernatural or extraterrestrial being. Their function is to introduce doubt/suspense into the story.

Nemesis – Unique, charismatic character with more negative than positive qualities. Functions are to make the hero/heroine look good and to create risks/obstacles/setbacks for the hero/heroine. Nemeses may also be forces of nature (diseases, predators, mental/physical challenges or supernatural beings).

Tricksters – Embody the energy of mischief and desire for change. They may provide comic relief or balance unrelieved tension, suspense and conflict. They are often a catalyst for change while remaining unchanged themselves.

Shadows – Represent the energy of the dark side – the unexpressed, unrealized, rejected or hidden side of a character. May also represent unexplored potential such as creativity or psychic ability. Shadows create conflict and bring out the best in the hero/heroine. Often depicted as monsters, demons, evil spirits or ghosts.

In your Great Story, try to create a balance of strengths and flaws between your Antagonist(s) and Protagonist(s) so that either one has a chance to overcome the other and/or to achieve their goals.

Not all Great Stories feature all or even most of these Iconic Characters or Archetypes. The only Character you must have is a **Protagonist** (a sentient being capable of thinking, feeling, acting and reacting to internal (thoughts/feelings) and external catalysts).

Your **Antagonist** can also be an institution (such as a government or a school), a life-threatening disease, being trapped by rising floodwaters, a moral dilemma (whether to lie or to tell the truth), etc.

Great Beginnings, Middles & Ends

Great Beginning...

1) Introduces Major Characters (such as protagonist, antagonist, etc.)

2) Hints at or shows Major Conflict(s) or Challenges Protagonists will face.

   Example: If your protagonist is an 8-year-old child and the challenge he/she faces is being lost in a wilderness, you could begin by showing him/her leaving the group he/she is hiking with for a reason that makes sense to the child.

3) Many Great Beginnings show the last significant event that occurs just before the actual story begins

4) Your **Goal** is to "Hook" or capture the attention of your potential audience. As is true in fishing, the more enticing and irresistible your bait is, the more fish you're going to hook and catch.

Great Middle

1) Try to make the middle of your story as entertaining and suspenseful as you can. Suspense is created by making the stakes for your protagonist as high as possible, by giving your readers, listeners and watchers important information that the protagonist does not yet have, and by giving tantalizing hints of the answers to the questions your audience is asking themselves about your story or your characters.

   Examples: If your protagonist is searching for stolen money, make the amount $1,000,000 instead of $100. If he/she witnesses a serious crime, the perpetrator might be a close friend, a lover, child, sibling or parent of the protagonist.

2) Each **Incident** must be connected to the **Incidents** that precede it and the **Incidents** that follow via **Cause** and **Effect.**

Great Endings

1) A **Great Ending** for any story must be a logical, natural and satisfying culmination to all of the previous **Incidents** in your story.

2) A **Great Ending** satisfies and rewards your audience, making them feel as if the time and attention they devoted to experiencing your story is worthwhile.

3) A **Great Ending** illustrates the **Theme** or **Moral** of your story.

   Example: If the theme of your story is: "Crime doesn't pay", then you would probably end it with your criminals being arrested and/or losing whatever they had stolen.

Exercises That Can Help You Become a Great Writer

1) Pick a favorite story to read, listen to or watch as a recording. If you pick something that is relatively short, the process will be easier and more enjoyable. When I did this exercise with *Romeo & Juliet,* I discovered that there

were at least 140 incidents in this great story.

2) Make a list of or write each incident on digital/actual notecards in the story you chose, in the order in which they happen.

An **Incident** is:

1) Any action(s) and/or reaction(s) performed by a **Character** or **Characters.**

2) Any interaction(s) between 2 or more **Characters** including face to face conversations and communication facilitated by technology (walkie-talkie, phones, skype, radios, etc.)

3) **Incidents** are motivated by an **External Catalyst** (a tornado touches down, receiving a phone call, a power failure or finding a bag of money) or an **Internal Catalyst** (waking up from a nightmare, having a vision, suddenly remembering something significant) which causes or motivates a **Character(s)** to take action or interact. **Catalysts** often serve as a bridge between **Incidents** in a Story.

Example: Interaction - R(omeo) tells J(uliet) he loves her when (**Catalyst)** he sees her on her balcony. Using initials instead of character's names will streamline this process.

Example: Action - People run out of a building screaming as (**Catalyst)** building shakes and crumbles in an earthquake.

Example: Reaction – S(usan) is watching TV when (**Catalyst**) a favorite song comes on. She jumps up, starts to dance and sing along with the music.

How Can You Adapt Any Story to Make it Your Own?

Setting – By changing the Time, Place and/or Location

Characters - By changing the Sex, Age, Species and/or the roles some of the characters play in your story. You may also choose to add, subtract or combine characters found in the original story if you think these changes will make your story more interesting and/or entertaining.

Incidents - By adding, changing, substituting or eliminating incidents. Be aware that making these changes may alter the structure and even the theme of the original version of the story, which you may not intend to do.

Theme - By changing/modifying the theme to one that is consistent with your own beliefs and values and any changes you've made in the incidents, characters and setting

Media - By changing the original media to one you most enjoy working in and/or one you think works best for your story.

Examples:

- *Romeo & Juliet*

  16th Century Verona

  Feuding Families

  Capulets/Montagues

  Priest (Ally, Friend)

  Stage Play

- *West Side Story*

  1950's New York City

  Rival Street Gangs

  Jets/Sharks

  Maria's girlfriend (Ally)

  Musical Play & Film

Theme is the same for both: True love transcends death.

How Can You Write Your Own Great Stories?

Exercise

1) Decide Who and What you want to Write About. Choosing something that has emotional significance for you will make telling this story easier, more enjoyable and satisfying.

2) **Examples:** Suppose that your loved one disappeared or was murdered, and that this crime was never solved, or that you have just retired from a successful career.

3) Make a list or jot down on note cards what you feel are the most significant

and interesting events in your story. This works best if you write down every possible incident you think you might want to include in your story.

4) If you intend to write a non-fiction story, please check and double check your facts.

5) If you're writing fiction, you will probably be using your imagination and life experiences more than any other source. If you want to fictionalize a true story, you may need to change the names, settings, professions, etc. of the people you are writing about to protect them and yourself from legal ramifications (being sued for slander, etc.).

Example: Depending upon the story you decide to tell, you may be using a variety of sources – your memories, journals, diaries, photographs, interviews with significant people, news stories, historical records, etc.

6) Once you have your list/note cards, try to number or arrange them into what you feel is the most entertaining

and interesting order, keeping in mind that you need a beginning, a middle and an end to your story. Please don't skip or rush this step. Play with the order of your incidents until you're satisfied. You will find that your list or cards arranged on a storyboard makes writing your story more fun, easier and faster.

7) As you do this exercise, you may be inspired to discard, add and/or combine incidents. Keep in mind that you must link each incident to the one preceding and following it.

8) This does not mean that you must tell your story in strict chronological order.

9) Sometimes it is more effective and entertaining to place an incident that happened before or after as a foreshadowing or a flashback.

Example: In your story you are driving along a country road on a foggy night. This reminds you of a frightening incident from your childhood (auto accident - flashback) and/or foreshadows a similar incident that will happen on this road later in your story.

10) Keep in mind that each incident must be consistent with your theme. If the theme of your story is "Good triumphs over evil" then your protagonist will defeat or overcome the antagonist in the end. Or you may discover that the theme of your story is actually "Old age and treachery overcome youth and enthusiasm every time." In this case the antagonist will defeat or overcome your protagonist.

Storytellers and Electronic Media

The days when a storyteller's only choice of media was to share his/her stories with family and friends around a campfire using voice, gestures, dance, facial expressions, simple instruments like drums or flutes and props (the spear he/she used to kill a mammoth that morning, for example) are long gone. And yet, we still use all of these forms of creative expression in live and recorded audio/video performances.

Technology is a double-edged sword. While it gives story tellers an ever expanding and evolving choice of media with which to share our creations, our potential audience has the same mind-numbing array of choices for entertainment, learning and diversion.

Another Fantasy Encounter with Abbott and Costello

Phil Silverman

(Fair Use of Trademarks deemed)

BUD: Well Lou! Can you believe it? We're moving up in the world!

LOU: We still live in Mr. Fields' rooming house.

BUD: Listen, in society, the lower you go the higher you go!

LOU: We're moving from the third floor to the first floor. How is that moving up?

BUD: (pushes Lou) We are going from room 311 to room 111. We are near the front entrance - you won't have to fight with Stinky on the stairwell!

LOU: If I'm going to visit Hillary upstairs, I'll take my chances!

BUD: Hey! This is a family show! Listen, pal, I was just trying to lift your spirits!

LOU: I lift my own spirits! I had two beers last night! But I still want an answer - How is moving down moving up?

BUD: When you move to the first floor, as I say, you're moving up!

LOU: How is that moving up?

BUD: It is, Lou!

LOU: How?

BUD: Existentially speaking, yes. (Takes cigarette puff).

LOU: (Aside to audience): On top of everything, he's gotta pull words on me!

BUD: Oh, I'm not pulling anything! Lou, calm down; let's just say when you move up, the world is your oyster!

LOU: Got a few pieces of shell in there, already!

BUD: (Loudly): Not necessary, is it? Ok (smiles), let me demonstrate to you that you've already taken on a more intellectual image; now you can give me an answer to this difficult civil service – test. Question: you're in an elevator.

LOU: No, I'm right here, what?

BUD: You're in an elevator; what floor do you want?

LOU: I want the first floor!

BUD: First floor? You're already on the first floor! With your new status you've got to be aware of your surroundings!

LOU: I still want the first floor!

BUD: Why, Lou?

LOU: That's where we moved to!

BUD: Good night, folks!

When They Cross the Border (Excerpts)
Lorraine Gow

CORNBREAD IN THE MORNING
When the sun pushes through the smog
in the one-bedroom house I call home,
it peeks through the cracks in the curtains,
telling all of us that we are safe;
the boogeyman bypassed our apartment,
heard Mama's prayers to Guadalupe,
smelled the novena candles,
watched for signs that we didn't give up,
succumbed to ghetto despair —
signals the American language
cues were missed,
signals we didn't understand,
uncomfortableness of the Old South,
deep in some hearts.

Police sirens and wild young men jumping
fences are left to the night's games,
for all mornings bring a chance
for the cycle to recycle,
for all us poor black Latinx,
but better off and yes,

we eat cornbread in the morning;
it's just that our bread is made from masa –
shaped round and flattened,
but my people called it tortilla.

THE ASPARAGUS ALARM CLOCK
I used to dream about Mama

reading fairy tales to me.

She'd highlight the parts where I was

supposed

to shake and CLOSE MY EYES,

but the alarm clock tic-tocked, tic-tocked too

early for blond-hair girl tales.

My Honduran Mama picked asparagus and

peas during tough times; she never played

CHESS,

And the hard times kept coming,

never a vacation or overtime pay.

You see, Mama didn't follow

ALICE down the rabbit hole;

Black immigrants followed no one,

not even dreams or nightmares.

Mama made an unfamiliar right turn

involving betrayals and tea parties.

And when the WHITE RABBIT said he was

late, Mama nodded – *yes*.

Her descent into madness began

with the birth of her sixth child.

No breast milk, no dry powdered milk,

no nothing to satisfy even a CHESHIRE CAT.

How does Mama cross a desert with

three live children and the memory of two?

The coyote's head was never taken,

only feared like the JABBERWOCKY.

"¡Págale al hombre!" "Pay the man!"

And Mama did with her eldest, Maria Ana.

She never liked that child anyway,

wanting to live beyond her color, her means!

Mama roamed avenues and boulevards

where the DOORMOUSE promised honey,

AND she peddled plastic bags of asparagus

–

four dollars, five dollars for organics.
I now cook asparagus for MAMA for free,
for lunch or for dinner or
for whenever she wants.

Senior Text-Back Symbols
Cheryl and Phil Silverman

For Men:
TBIM
Text back, it moved
TBIWFATHIOF
Text back, I'm watching Football and the house is on fire

For Women:
TBIAPS
Text back, I'm at Payless Shoes
TBIES
Text back, I'm exchanging shoes

For both:
TBILMI
Text back, I lost my iPhone
TBIIAROWIWD
Text back, I'm in a restaurant ordering water I won't drink
TBIHSRTM
Text back, I have stopped reading text messages

A Longing for Buzz

Barbara DeMarco-Barrett

One June when I was in my early twenties, my best friend and I left the suburbs of Philadelphia for the hills of West Virginia to spend the summer with friends of hers she met at a commune in Taos, New Mexico. Ten days after we arrived in West Virginia, I spent a weekend at a crafts fair selling handmade jewelry—how I made my money in those days—which is where I met Tony, a sizzling hot hippie dude who crafted handmade furniture from rosewood. We were attracted to each other like honeybees to clover.

When the fair ended, Tony invited me to stay at his cabin in a nearby holler. The cabin sat in an idyllic setting, surrounded by trees and wildlife. It was my summer to try new things, so I said, why not?

Tony parked his truck near his work shed off the highway. I carried my backpack and tote filled with my journal and books—*Be Here Now, The Dharma Bums, A Movable Feast*—and followed him down a dirt path to a clearing where there sat a cabin built with repurposed barn wood.

"Here it is," he said, gesturing widely, as if this was a castle and not a one-room cabin without electricity or plumbing. The cabin was clean, but it was unfinished. As in, in process. The cardboard insulation would eventually be covered with knotty pine, and if I hadn't been ensconced in the fog of lust, I would have cared a little bit more about home design.

Tony had a six-pack before they were called that, eyes green as lime juice, and talented hands, especially when we were together. He told me he escaped a bad marriage in Brooklyn and a job at his family's restaurant and moved here to work the land.

"My wife went out with my best buddy," he said in his West Virginia drawl, no hint of Brooklyn anywhere, "and I decided right then and there to leave that life and stop thinking. I couldn't make sense out of what happened, but the land doesn't betray you."

I couldn't imagine what thinking had to do with cheating wives, but I was astounded. He'd never strung together so many words at one time. It gave me hope that there was a thinker and talker beneath his reticent but hot exterior.

After a tour of the property, he showed me how to fetch water from the well, how to start a cook fire with twigs and a match, and how to roll the perfect cigarette using Bugler tobacco. All of it was new to me, so different from my life in Philly.

Just before sunset my first night there, Tony and I sat on the stoop by the open door.

"Lookie there," he said, and put down his whittling. I closed my book. Behind a grove of birch trees, the setting sun cast a golden honeyed light. Leaves edged with gold. As he lit a hand-rolled cigarette, a great hum filled the air as if just beyond the trees, musicians tuned their instruments. Tony didn't notice. How could he not notice?

A moment later an orderly swarm of honeybees arced over us and into an opening in the cardboard wall beside the bed. Tony puffed on the ciggie. I froze.

When the last bee disappeared into the wall, I said, "What the hell was that?"

"They was bees," he said. "You ain't going crazy."

"Do they stay in there all night?"

"Yep," he said. "In the mornin' they leave to do their work pollinating flowers."

"They're in there all night, then." I'd never heard of humans and bees co-existing like this.

"All night," he said, as if it was the most natural thing.

My heart jitterbugged against my rib cage. "I'm afraid of bees."

"Then I guess you best get over it fast." He took a puff of the hand-rolled and handed it to me.

Fifteen minutes later what had sounded like an orchestra became a vague hum that soothed my ears, like the ocean at night or birds in the woods.

As if living with bees wasn't bad enough, I had to make my way in the dark to the bathroom, a weedy area one hundred feet away.

"Any wild animals out there?" I asked.

"Just some garter snakes in the beyond. They tuck in early."

I grabbed the roll of toilet paper by the door and headed out. "If I'm not back in 10 minutes, call 9-1-1."

He let go a laugh. "You're funny. We don't have a phone."

As I ambled along the dirt path, night sounds accompanied me—a rustling in the bushes, an owl's hooting. I wondered what I'd gotten myself into. No phone … a bathroom in the weeds … snakes in the beyond … bees.

When I returned, I rinsed my hands in the wash bucket outside the door. Back inside, I read a little longer by candlelight as Tony polished a newly carved stool. Then he blew out the candle and pulled me to him. He smelled like the rosewood he used in his woodworking.

The next morning Tony went to work in the shed by the road while his donkey, Harold, and I headed for the general store down the hill. I held onto the reins, learned to pull this way or that to move him in a certain direction. Harold's back felt solid and warm beneath me and he smelled like hay. He maintained a slow, steady gait as we moseyed along at two mph. The clomp-clomp of hooves and the music of songbirds made me understand how this lifestyle and these hills could grow on you. One pickup truck passed us during our forty-five-minute trip to the store, a contrast to the mad rush of the southeastern Pennsylvania expressways. A squirrel dashed across the gravel road. Two bunnies darted haphazardly by, and a cardinal alighted on a branch, its red feathers signaling something, but what? I hoped it meant good things were in store for me here in the holler.

At the store I packed the side-bags with eggs, apples, milk, flour, and beans, and Harold and I trekked back up the hill, moving through the woods, passing under horse chestnut trees, mulberries, and spruces a thousand shades of green. Those four hours were the high point of my stay, but how would I feel if I did this all the time, how long it would take to grow tired of spending so much time with Harold acquiring groceries.

One surprising thing happened: I grew unafraid of the bees and began looking forward to them. Their arrival tested my mettle, as did cooking with wood, hauling water from the well, and living without anything extraneous. I could live without *stuff*, but I could not live without books, without connection, without people.

One morning Tony and I hiked to a lookout point where hills and trees stretched for miles. There was no denying the pristine beauty of what lay before us, but it left me feeling empty.

"Don't you think the view'd be better if there were a house or church or something plopped in there to contrast all that natural beauty?" I said.

"It's paradise the way it is," he said. "Don't worry—you'll grow to love the holler, too."

"I hope so," I said, but already I could see that Tony's idea of country living, and mine, were about as far apart as fresh-picked peaches and fruit in the can.

If only we talked about books and writing, on which I'd become more and more dependent. Tony's reading material extended to owners' manuals for woodworking equipment.

One day I returned from picking berries to find Tony sitting by the fire-pit absorbed in a book. This excited me, like finding an overlooked gift under the Christmas tree.

I sat in one of his sculpted hand-carved chairs. "What're you reading?"

"This is pure poetry, darlin'," he said. "Listen to this," and he proceeded to read me a passage about how to make box joints with a router.

Chemistry lasts only so long when the brain disengages.

A week later I asked Tony to drive me back to my friends—not because of the bees or lack of plumbing or electricity but because I needed to talk about something other than crops or wood.

It wasn't the last time I got involved with the wrong guy, but it *was* the summer I realized books and writing were more important than I knew. I returned to college with a dedication to writing that would last throughout my life, as would my fondness for bees.

Orange County
Cheryl Silverman

Live in Orange County;
Really love the green terrain
and the sunny skies

Love: I Love the Way She Loves

Beth Cornelius

 I was anticipating Zooming time. It was only a half hour away! I opened a new book of mine and thought about my dear sister who started a Zooming time with our singing group and began a separate Zooming time for our families. The words on the page talked about love! And I thought, *I love the way my sister loves! She loves in so many ways.* I was so impressed by what I read about love that I even read the page aloud during our Zoom session.

My sister's Zooming has put our faraway families in the den of her Laguna Woods home! And what a loving place that is! Songs, shared stories, and laughter fill the zoom room. Prior to the family Zoom sessions, many family members across the country were seldom seen; now they also share in the fun of Zooming!

Hey! It sure is a good thing my family is so easy to love because of their caring ways. It makes loving them so effortless! But even with family members I love, sometimes it is easy to get irritated. But what if my family members were mean and uncaring? Would I still love them? YES! Yes, I would love them anyway because they are family, but it would take an effort.

It is a choice to love! Striking back is so easy! But choosing not to, could save a friendship or even a marriage, and maybe even your job. Unbelievable as it may seem, letting go of perceived or real offenses brings a life of peace!

The human spirit can rise to this higher plane, but I find it a boost to raise a cry for help to God because I believe that He supplies added strength to honor each other and do the right thing!

One way we can cultivate love is to make our homes safe havens where warmth and caring really show up shining! We can choose not to say negative words that come to mind. We can ask ourselves, "Is there another way of saying what's bothering me without using toxic words?" Then we can choose to say words of honor, respect, and love!

I'm so thankful that my sister knows so much about computers and Zooming! She has brought our families, who live so far away, together! Now, that is love and it is so wonderful! I love the way she loves! I truly do! And yes, you might know her, and you might have felt her love; her name is Sunshine.

Foolish Me / I Need Me So

Phil Silverman

(After-hours, soft ballad,
retro-Billie Holiday style)

Note to non-musicians: The letters and
numbers (C6) represent musical notation for
guitar, ukulele, or piano.

Foolish Me

C6   F6
He was smart
C6
But not smart enough
F6
When it came to my kids.
C6
Yeah, he could be a little rough;
F6
Came from the "old school"
C6
Don't take no "guff."
Dmi   G7
Now I see

G7   F   G7   C
Foolish me, Foolish me.

```
        C6    F6
    His jokes were funny
            C6
    But just a little stale.
            F6
    He smoked his stogie
            C6
    Said he didn't inhale.
            F6
    Kept the unsmoked half
            C6
    Overnight next to the kale.
            Dmi
        Now I see
    G7      F   G7      C
    Foolish me, Foolish me.


            F
Refused to seek his feminine side
            F
    Or tell our son
            F
    It's okay to cry.


        Bb
Wasn't with the program;

    Didn't get it;
```

C
Couldn't see.

(spoken) I wonder if he sits alone and says
G7   G7
"Foolish me"?

© PLS 2009

<u>I Need Me So</u>

If there was a way to tell me
Just what I know I mean to me
And it's clear to me
There's no fear for me
to express the necessity –
I need me so.

If I could articulate
Just what I need it to let me know
And certainly, it must show
That inward glow,
I must express the necessity –
I need me so.

I need me when I'm dreaming
Of iridescent, early morning scenes;
I need me when in the beaming
The wanting to be near

Me.
Craving for the power
That pungent puff of cool repose,
Waiting for the hour
Of warmly, 'borning lost control.

If there was a way to tell me
Just what I want to know,
And it's clear to me
…No fear to be
Expressive of necessity
To Need Me So.

© PLS 1973

Black and Yellow
Nancy Brown

While black and yellow wouldn't be my first choice of color combinations for much of anything, it has come to have a special significance in my life. In elementary school, I rode a black and yellow bus to school every day with my best friends, Karen and Wendy. Some of the prettiest butterflies I've ever seen were black and yellow while one of the most frightening insects, a bumble bee, also called a yellow jacket, took out its vengeance on Mom. That's when she learned that she was allergic to bees, ended up in the hospital and wore a medic alert bracelet the rest of her life for that possible, life-threatening, allergic reaction. At age 16, my first car, a 1952 Chevy that I paid a whopping $150 for, had a black and yellow license plate. In California, that was the only choice in 1961. I never really thought much about any of this until much later.

When I graduated from high school and went off to college, my school colors were none other than black and yellow. LOTS of it! My flag twirler uniform, t-shirts, marques, book covers, even the alumni letters I still receive 53 years later, were all black and yellow! When I went to my 50th high school reunion, I decided to head to the bookstore where I found a license plate frame that read **Alumni—Cal State LA.** Perfect!

Living in Alaska from 1994-2005, black and yellow showed up along the way throughout my journey in the Last Frontier. From the time I learned to drive, I always seemed to have a "lead foot," my not-so-wonderful habit of driving too fast. It wasn't very long after I arrived in Anchorage that I discovered a school sign that seemed to appear out of nowhere. The 45-mph speed limit at the bottom of the hill turned to 35 mph in the blink of an eye, then to 25 mph around the corner at the top of a hill. I soon learned from the nice man in uniform that there was a school nearby. Somehow, I felt compelled to argue my plight in traffic court on more than one occasion. This time, I pleaded passionately with the judge, "I'm new to the area, don't know my way around, and certainly feel victimized by that school sign I had no clue was there." I soon learned that in Alaska drivers only have six chances within a two-year period to make mistakes on the road before they lose their license. Although I thankfully never reached that threshold, I was keenly aware of that possibility as the days, weeks and months ticked away. Guess

I needed to be on the lookout for black and yellow signs with the words "SCHOOL," "SLOW/Children Playing" or "CAUTION."

Yellow and black followed me on to Illinois where I spent ten years following my retirement from the Anchorage School District. I never tired of the beauty of Alaska, but Illinois was another story. No mountains. No ocean. And flat. That meant no local skiing, one of my greatest passions in life. I was determined to find something beautiful about that state after leaving the incredibly gorgeous scenery of Alaska. Nature has a way of finding me as if to say, "Here I am! Beauty is in the eyes of the beholder!" I soon discovered huge, beautiful sunflowers that covered the fields behind the house where I first lived in the Land of Lincoln proudly displaying their colors. Or did they find me? "A banana a day keeps the doctor away," a twist on the "an apple a day" saying soon became part of my daily routine. Having been a teacher most of my adult life, black and yellow appeared throughout my math classes in the form of student rulers, pencils and even smiley faces.

Although I loved to ski since discovering my passion for the sport when I turned 30 after living in cold climates for 21 years, I concluded that I didn't want to shovel snow when I was 80 years old. The pull to return to California got stronger and stronger, so in December 2015 I made the bold move to return to California where I was born and raised. A trip to my local DMV resulted in a new driver's license and registration. At first, I just got the generic license plate. Later, however, it occurred to me to sign up for a special plate in, what else, black and yellow. I decided to go a step further and get it personalized...

FL CRCL

I wonder what other "black and yellow" surprises await me in my remaining lifetime journeys...

Grace Notes
William Scott Galasso

Hillside wind stirs lacey leaves
of pepper trees, small birds
flutter in branches,

a lizard navigates red brick
slightly uneven as all things
man-made, and we sip

plum purple wine inhaling
notes of earth, subtle spice
I cannot place but know

tasting cherries, chocolate
a hint of cassis and I
crave nothing, need less

watching falcons glide
under white clouds, blue skies
over harvest time vineyards

'til my fingers touch hers reflexively
this woman loved for forty years,
and I savor the wondrous Now.

(Previously published in Summer 2021
California Quarterly, Vol 47.2)

A Wedding to Forget
Jerry Schur

There we were in the chapel, the Reverend Hopnagel, Janellen, my rich, somewhat unattractive, and occasionally bitchy bride and me, plus the Bouncer and about one hundred guests. I must add that Janellen was slightly pregnant, not by my hand or any other part of my anatomical construction. To relax, I had taken several glasses of Pinot Noir a few minutes earlier. Five glasses, to be exact. Large glasses. I did feel relaxed. I heard the Reverend saying, "for better or for worse." Then he paused and looked at me.

"For better," I said.

'No," said Reverend Hopnagel smiling benignly. "You must say 'I do.'"

"You said for better or for worse. I choose better."

"Dammit," said Janellen. "Just say 'I do.'"

"Yes, 'I do'," said the Bouncer. He was Janellen's father. I called him the Bouncer because he always bragged that that was his first job. He never told me how he made his considerable sums of money after that.

The Reverend nodded, still smiling. "I do," he prompted.

"No," I said. "The word 'or' is disjunctive. Either, or. You gave me a choice. I chose better."

The good Reverend Hopnagel was still smiling as he nervously ran a finger under his collar. "Just say 'I do', please."

"Just say it," said the less than lovely Janellen, quite angry. "For chrissakes, you buffoon, just say it."

"Say it," said The Bouncer in a threatening voice.

"Look," I told them. "I am a high school English teacher. I understand grammar. Given the choice, I choose better."

"What should I do?" asked the bewildered Reverend.

"What the hell," said the snarling Janellen.

"Last chance," said the Bouncer.

"I will not begin my marriage by debasing the precise meaning of words or by ignoring rules of grammar which I…"

Before I could continue, The Bouncer had punched me on the jaw. "Say 'I do' damn you," he shouted in a voice which could easily be heard in the back pews.

Janellen called me a dirty name. I can't say it, but I'll give you a hint. It begins with 'ass' and ends with 'hole'.

The Reverend Hopnagel said, "Hit him again." The Bouncer did.

That's how I lost my bride, my consciousness and one tooth. But I kept my honor, and I can look each student in the eye when I teach the disjunctive.

Big Bang

S. Ramagopal

Muir

More

Moor

A(o)bstra(u)ct

Murky

Muddy

Heady

Freezing -- Roasting
Sunshine Lutey

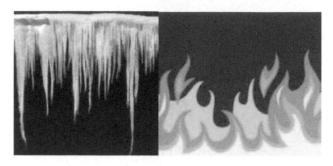

I think many couples may have very different metabolisms David and I surely do. When David returned home after being away, I wanted nothing more than to snuggle with him in bed; but he was freezing, and I was roasting.

The couple

Snuggling in bed
Hubby pulls covers tight
Wife says, "I can't breathe!"
But her heart says, "Let me snuggle!"

Feet burning up
Push and pull covers
10 minutes ago
Feet felt like ice!

Feet hanging out
Free at last!
Got to turn over
Snuggles needed, but body rebels!

The Grandparents

Grandma opens the window,
Grandpa slams it shut.
Hm-m-m-m
Maybe we're related?

The couple

Our comfort zone
Seventy-Eight degrees
Grown children at the door
Quick turn on the air.

Children go out the door
Hubby says
"Quick, turn off that air
I'm freezing."

The wife

Freezing in hotel room
Set temp to 78°
Roasting; set temp to 74°
Freezing -- Repeat

The couple

Hubby home from the hospital
Says, "I'm freezing;
Make it 80°
Wife got naked.

Bedtime; wife tucks hubby in
Sets temp to 74°
Climbs in uncovered
Reaches in – comfortable snuggle.

The Old Red Brick Building: Lal Hebeli
Daya Shankar-Fischer

Note for the readers: On the high level of the Himalayan foothills was the gorgeous resort of Messouri and down in the valley of the Himalayan foothills was the city of Dehradun. In the city was a cluster of old houses and in the middle of these houses stood an Old Red Brick Building (The Lal Hebeli).

The city of Dehradun is situated near the foothills of the Himalayan Mountains in the state of Uttaranchal in India. Nearby Dehradun up high in the mountains are many vacation resorts; among them the most popular one is Messouri. Every summer thousands of vacationers, particularly the rich and famous, would come to Messouri to find refuge from the scorching summer heat of the lower plains.

The spectacular Himalayan Mountains offer a gorgeous view from the valley below, which has a tranquil breeze.

Under the British Raj, the Messouri vacation resort received special attention because the British were really charmed by its gorgeous mountain views. The magical mountain peaks often touched by the roaming clouds, the beautiful sunrise and the magnificent sunset, and the hills covered with a bed of colorful wildflowers would make it an irresistible place for visitors.

The British diplomats made Messouri even more inviting by adding the gardens, bath houses, massage parlors, and the beautiful residential bungalows. The luxury of having personal servants, gardeners, and cooks made Messouri a very special summer resort. Every summer the British diplomats travel hundreds of miles to experience the life of luxury -- Messouri.

Traveling on narrow and rugged mountain roads was extremely difficult. Even the most sophisticated means of transportation were not a match for some of the very treacherous rough, hilly roads. Only the natives, who are known as the mountain people, were able to climb these rugged roads. The bone-chilling winds from the snow-covered mountain peaks could be brutal. Often even the natives would be subject to serious accidents, injuries, and even death.

For the natives, transporting cargo and tourists on hand-driven rickshaws was their means of earning a living. They would travel from the valley to the mountains, pulling the rickshaws with bare hands and almost bare feet, except some wore worn out flip flops.

So often they would slip and get foot or back injuries. Shortness of breath, congested lungs, coughing, and pneumonia were common health problems for these poor mountain dwellers. There was no hospital, clinic or doctor in sight. The natives work so hard, taking life-threatening risks for very little pay. That was the life for the natives, the mountain dwellers.

The people who lived in the valley of the Himalayan hills had lived there for generations. There were clusters of old homes but they were very well maintained by their owners. In the middle of these homes stood one very old building – the red brick building – known as the Lal Hebeli.

The Dr. Anand family inherited the red brick building-Lal Hebeli. This had been the residence of the Anand family for several generations.

Dr. Anandji had a very nice family. A beautiful wife Asha, Hope, and their two children: a son, Nirbhaya-the fearless, and a daughter Beer Bala-the brave one (Bala for short).

For Dr. Anandji, inheriting the Lal Hebeli perfectly fulfilled his life's dream – to open a free clinic for the mountain people, the natives of Himalayan Hills.

The red brick building appeared to be telling its story in silence. From its chipped paint, falling mortar, and half crushed bricks one could easily guess that it was an old…a very old building that had weathered the cold, harsh, and persistent winter storms. They swept down from the high and rough terrain of the Himalaya Mountains to the valley.

Dr. Anandji chose the main floor of this building to open the clinic for the oppressed. His patients knew him as "Dr. Ji" of Lal Hebeli.

He designated the morning hours, the peak hours of his medical practice to treat only the poor and the oppressed. Anyone who could not afford the medical treatment at other places would come to Lal Hebeli to get a free checkup, free medication, and emergency treatment.

Each morning, even before dawn, patients would be waiting at the big old gate of Lal Hebeli. As the old gate would begin to open, there would be the big roar from the sound of greetings from the crowd. After "Namaste Doctor Ji," the patients would enter his office one by one. This was the routine at the Lal Hebeli every day of the week.

It was very difficult for the neighbors as they watched the long lines of wounded or sick patients every day; somehow, they tolerated it. But some cases were particularly sad to see, such as the mother who carried a sick young baby in her lap. The baby was clinging to her mother's bosom, so weak that she could hardly move. The nurses at the clinic would see such scenes and whisper, "How nice of Doctor Anandji to open this place at Lal Hebeli.

The gatekeeper, Shamu, would open the main gate of the Red Brick Building at dawn, about 6:00 a.m., for the long line of waiting patients. Ramu, the dedicated compounder, would prepare the waiting room for the patients. However, even before the main gate would open, a long line of patients would be waiting at the door of Lal Hebeli Clinic.

Ramu did not look forward to this extremely difficult duty of the Clinic though he had been a dedicated clinic supervisor for several years.

Still there would be times that he would question his strength, stamina, and patience to cope with such crises.

One foggy Monday morning when the visibility was only about a few feet, a man named Sarju entered the clinic with bruises all over his body. Both of his eyes were bloodshot and partially closed; he could hardly see anything. The people standing in line probably thought he was a rickshaw driver who had rolled down the steep hills.

Surju was in pain, but he patiently waited for Dr. Anandji. The hardships of life had prepared him to bear the pains. He had an unwavering faith and hope that somehow Dr. Anandji would take care of his wounds and the pain would go away. Dr. Anandji came and looked at Surju; his wounds looked terrible, and his swollen eyes were almost closed. Dr. Anandji had learned to be calm, even when he faced some very seriously injured patients. He calmly checked Surju's wounds and wrote a little note of instructions to the nurse on how to take care of Surju's wounds and instructed the nurse to get some pain pills from the dispensary in the next room in the Lal Hebeli.

Outside the clinic the waiting line continued to get longer. Though the rule at the clinic was one patient at a time, three or four patients were pushing to get inside. It would get chaotic and noisy, but that was not unusual and did not disturb the doctor. His focus was to treat as many patients as he could.

Magi, the British nurse said to the compounder, "I am not sure if I can take it. I may leave."

"Well, this is the way this clinic runs."

"But there is no order; it's very disorderly, chaotic, and very traumatic," said Magi.

"How come you came here Magi?"

"Well, I would often watch the scenes at the clinic as I would take my morning stroll. So, I felt a need to help and offered my services. Everyone welcomed me. Dr. Anandji is appreciative of my help."

"But Magi, the reality is that for these Mountain natives there is hardly any order in life. For them there is no escape from risks, danger, trauma, bruises, and hurt."

One day a patient named Chandu showed up at Lal Hebeli. He could not walk but was able to crawl to the Lal Hebeli clinic.

His hands were bruised badly so it was extremely difficult for him to reach the clinic's front door, but he came to the back door and came inside. The nurse Magi on duty did not like Chandu's coming in like this. That was against the rules. But looking at his condition and his teary eyes, Magi let him in. She helped him raise his body and placed him on a bench. As Magi was washing Chandu's wounds Dr. Anandji entered the room. He did not question Chandu's coming in from the back door, rather he asked, "Hey what happened? Have you been drinking again?"

"No doctor, it was my father who was drunk, I had an argument with him; he was hitting my little brother. I tried to stop him. He began to hit me and kept pushing me down the hill. I kept rolling down Chestnut Hill until I reached near the rock on that steep hill," said Chandu.

Dr. Anandji kept taking care of Chandu's wounds with the help of Magi. He did not pay much attention to Chandu's story. Because he had heard many stories like this one from his other patients. His main focus was to treat his wounds.

Dr Anandji opened this clinic that was not an orderly place. It may not have been well organized, but this clinic of the **Old Red Brick Building** served the most oppressed people in the Himalayan foothills in the state of Uttrachal-India.

Mientes – You Lie

Peggy P. Edwards

King Drew Magnet High School opened in 1982 as a medical/science high school designed to meet the needs of under-represented young people, with an interest in medicine and science in south-central Los Angeles.

Soon after I was hired to teach Spanish in 1998, I was called into the assistant principal's office for school orientation. She told me that these students were not particularly interested in learning Spanish, but they did plan to continue their studies at a university, and two years of a foreign language were required, as were good grades.

I devised the perfect plan which would accomplish my goal of teaching them Spanish and their goal of being accepted at a university.

I would start each class session with music, performed by trending musical icons such as Enrique Iglesias, Selena, Ricky Martin and Shakira. I prepared by having a stereo disc player installed in my classroom, as well as purchasing a variety of CDs by popular, Spanish-singing artists.

As planned, each class started with a song. The students were soon singing and dancing to the songs. Requisite grammar lessons accompanied the required memorization of that week's chosen song.

In my opinion, it was copacetic. The students appeared to be genuinely enjoying learning Spanish and my method of teaching it. Outsiders were amazed when they heard my students singing in Spanish outside the classroom.

But not all were happy. One morning, as the Enrique Iglesias' song "Miente — Dime que me amas" (Lie to Me -- Tell me that you love me) ended, Carla White spoke up.

"Mrs. Edwards, we don't like the way you teach Spanish. It's a waste of our time and we are not learning Spanish."

I pointed at her and said, "Mientes."

She replied, "I am not lying."

The entire class had stopped and heard the exchange. With that, the music and the lessons continued. We all realized that music is the perfect mnemonic. And to prove it, we ended the year by singing our songs in Spanish in the King Drew Medical Magnet auditorium. Our show was a favorite and enjoyed by all.

What greater proof that music can and does change the world and make it a better place? I do believe music has the power to save our world.

Fermata
Ellyn Maybe

Facebook is the obituary section of a
newspaper; I didn't realize I subscribed to it.

Sometimes I'm getting the news years after
they're gone.

Memories on the tip of the tongue.

Decades ago, lives in other cities, countries.
Sometimes immediately but still in the past
like a celluloid scrim marquee with capital
letters and small breath.

Remembering some moment in time before
clocks drifted their sands across eternity.

Condolences is the language filling the air
with a residue of music and dictionaries full of
pictures and time stopping glimpses into the
cities left behind.

The empty theater seats
with a ghost light beaming.
The violin with an elegy note
hanging in the air.

A Gift to Myself
Marcia C. Hackett

The very best thing I ever did for myself was to spend $3,000 *per eye* before cataract surgery to have special multifocal lenses implanted. If I had not made the decision prior to each operation, Medicare would have paid for generic lenses to be inserted at no extra cost. In that case, I would *still* have had to wear reading glasses afterwards. My two separate eye operations took place a year apart, as the left eye's cataract was not "ripe," the physician explained. In other words, the cataract was not ready for removal. I cannot begin to count the number of times I've related my story to folks planning on having this type of surgery, encouraging them not to be fearful and to consider similar action to mine. I am so grateful for my excellent vision and for the implants that improved my entire life.

The beginnings of blurriness in my sight happened about fifteen years ago. I had always had good vision, being farsighted, not needing glasses, especially for reading until after age 60. I was a teacher, spending much class time at the white board, writing or explaining the lesson, constantly taking off my reading glasses or putting them on so I could see up close. I also tried contact lenses and had much difficulty putting them in. One lens even broke in my eye causing a serious infection. So, if possible, I did not want to wear any type of glasses. My surgeon said that as we age, our sight begins to diminish. Pollsters estimate that nine out of ten Americans get cataracts by age 65, the most common eye ailment along with astigmatism.

A cataract can be best described as a cloudy film that develops over several years on the retina, impairing one's vision. Some folks may not even be aware of the symptoms at first, just crediting partial loss of sight due to aging.

Modern day cataract surgery is common, generally safe with little risk, and has a high success rate. Patients must get a medical diagnosis for the procedure which is done on an outpatient basis. A laser is used to remove the cataract which is replaced by artificial silicon, plastic or acrylic lens. The procedure takes less than an hour. Certain risks such as infection, inflammation and bleeding can occur, all of which vary with the individual. Recovery time is generally short with little discomfort, especially if one follows the doctor's orders such as putting in eye drops for several days. If all goes well, the implanted lens may never need to be replaced!

The true blessing of successful cataract surgery is the transformational effect on one's vision which becomes clearer. I can attest this truly happened to me. Without this operation, all aspects of one's daily life can be affected - driving, working, reading, etc. Researchers have found that many folks who had the surgery wish they had done it sooner. That was not my case. I contacted the eye surgeon as soon as my ophthalmologist said my cataracts were ready to be removed. Both my parents and paternal grandfather died almost blind from cataracts. All three of them, fearing the operation, refused to have it. Dad's favorite pastime was reading the *New York Times* which he was unable to do in the last ten years of his life. His father, who lived with us, loved the Brooklyn Dodgers. I often saw him in the living room, leaning over the radio, listening to the Dodger games, unable to watch them on television.

The cost for the surgery has undoubtedly gone up since I had mine, and will depend on one's insurance, individual health situation, and physician. I had no vision insurance and little extra money at the time of my procedures. Fortunately, my surgeon allowed me to pay for the cost of each eye over a 12-month period with no interest charges if I kept to the bargain. I did. For those contemplating the surgery, there is a wealth of information online about the procedure. Also, many eye surgery centers have their own web page describing their practice. My successful surgery has allowed me to enjoy excellent eyesight for the past fifteen years with no need for reading glasses. The only aftereffect is that due to having light blue eyes which are sensitive to bright sunlight, I need to wear sunglasses when outdoors – a small price to pay for my precious vision.

An addendum: At my annual complete vision test in July 2021 my eye doctor said I have "spectacular vision" and am "very blessed to have it at my age." I'm so grateful for the operations in 2008 and 2009.

Gypsy Wind
William Scott Galasso

This is not a summer breeze
grazing skin, tousling baby's
fine head of hair, nor is it breath
sloughing dew from sunflowers

or beads of rain on orange lantana.
It does not inspire lullabies,
Freshen air, whisper soliloquies or
Promise sleep to troubled minds.

No. This is wind, fulsome, moaning,
rapacious to leaves, whipping sand,
winnowing stalks of corn,
cracking branches, cleaving nests from trees.

This is a brawling wind whitening waves,
blackening clouds,
scoring chips of paint from old wooden barns,
snapping flags like towels,

powering weathervane's whirling madness,
prompting plate-shifts,
birthing tsunamis; this is a universe
reshaping itself.

(Previously published in California Quarterly,
Summer 2021 Vol 47.2)

Hell's Bells
Jon Perkins

Bruno Sedgwick looked the part of a Caltech mathematician, mainly because his eyebrows were a bushy black rat's nest. His round face and slightly protruding brown eyes gave him a distinctive air of brooding focus, although that was an unintended deception. Much of Bruno's time in thought was devoted to a slightly off-center sense of humor, which in the end would prove to be his undoing.

His part of a project to glean telemetric data from a Mars probe was a straightforward set of code meant to analyze shades of light bouncing off soil samples. It was so straightforward that Bruno felt offended by the simplicity of the task assigned to him. In consequence, he allowed his humor to hold sway by adding a subroutine designed to lure any extraterrestrials around to respond to a question he posed in code. Thus far, SETI, the search for extraterrestrial intelligence, had been a fruitless enterprise and Bruno saw no harm in adding his two-cents worth.

Bruno's subroutine invited a response to pi, the endless non-repetitive sequence of numbers following 3.14159…, in which case the response would add the next six digits in sequence. In so doing, the response would trigger an audio bell that would sound a 'ding,' like a reception desk summons for a bellhop.

The telemetry was returned to Pasadena in a room occupied by Bruno and his cohort of six other engineers and mathematicians, managed by stern-faced Fred Benton, an insufferable Nobel Laureate in chemistry. Fred regarded Bruno's frequent attempts at humor as proof of the man's idiocy.

The initial return of data went as expected, with rich information regarding the Red Planet's makeup, as well as some very interesting atmospheric details suggesting water whose volume changed with the Martian seasons.

All of a sudden, the room was filled with the sound of a bell ringing which instantly sent a flood of adrenaline into Bruno's stomach. Then, adding to Bruno's surprise, the bell clanged repeatedly in a deafening din.

"What the hell!" Fred exclaimed. He put his hands to his ears.

"Douse the noise!" he shouted.

Someone with sense cut the audio while Fred scanned the faces in the room, searching for the offender. It took him less than a second to fix his gaze on the hapless Bruno, still in a state of shock from the sound of the bell. He knew that it signaled an intelligent response, for the very first time confirming the existence of intelligent life elsewhere in the cosmos. He realized that he alone was responsible for this astonishing discovery.

"Bruno?" Fred asked in an exasperated voice. "Is that you again with your strange attempt at humor?"

"Yes!" Bruno replied in an anxious voice. "It was my idea to construct a test for the possibility of intelligent life on Mars!"

"Hogwash!" Fred replied. "What nonsense!" These words were accompanied by the sounds of snickering from the other scientists in the room.

"No. It's true. There's an intelligent being out there who recognized the test and responded!"

"Insanity!"

"It's true."

Fred pondered, never letting his eyes leave those of Bruno Sedgwick. In a few moments his face relaxed and his voice was lowered. "If it's true, Bruno, there would be proof in your code."

"Yes. Of course."

"Bring it to us. The others will want to take a gander as well." There were murmurs of assent.

Bruno hurried from the room. As he departed, he heard the voices of the others in a confused patter of skeptical ridicule.

Some minutes later, Bruno returned with his subroutine in hand, about twenty pages of computer printout comprising lines of code unintelligible to all but a few of those remaining in the room. He spread the papers out on a table soon surrounded by eight pairs of hunched eyes scanning the lines of code.

Finally, Fred stood, a look of disgust on his face. "What's to see, Bruno? It's obvious, isn't it?"

Bruno was shocked anew. He couldn't believe his eyes. The code had changed. It wasn't the code he'd written. Instead, it was a simple series of commands that rang the bell, triggered by an innocuous time-lapse of the telemetric data readout.

"You others," Fred said, "Stay here and go over the data. Without," he said wryly, "the confounded bell." He looked at Bruno. "You come with me. We have things to discuss."

As he followed Fred from the room, Bruno couldn't help but understand something about the alien out there. It shared his sense of humor.

.

The Story of Mary, Mother of Jesus
Daneen Pysz

Matthew 1 & 2, Luke 1:26-56,
Luke 2:1-52, Luke 3:23-38

(Jesus is writing to his Mom)

Dad said it was time.
Mankind needed their Savior.
A promise is a promise
and Scripture must be fulfilled.

It took 42 generations for the
perfect Mom to bring me to this world.
Little did she know that she was the one!
The blessed one!
To have the Messiah as her son!
Isaiah prophesied it so many years ago.

Joachim & Anna were her parents.
Faithful and old, they had no children.
Pouring their hearts out to God,
An angel tells them
their prayers are answered.

They pledge their only child to the Lord.
When Mary's three,
she is dedicated to the temple.
Just like Hannah did with Samuel.

At 12 years of age, decisions must be made
for this virgin's life.

"Come one, come all: Single men and
Widowers of our nation."
Lay down your staff so priests
can pray for a sign from God.
How will we know who is the one?
A dove lands on Joseph. This is the sign.
No love involved; Joe is the chosen one.

Much older and with sons,
Joseph takes Mom to his home.
Telling her, "I must leave to build homes,
Mary; but I'll be back soon.
The Lord will protect you."
Courageous Mom, in a strange home with
stepsons close to her age to care for.

My Mother's faith is strong
as she serves our Heavenly Father.
Continuing to weave purple and scarlet
thread for the Veil of God's Temple.
Always patiently watching and praying,
Watching and praying.
She lives her life in purity for our Heavenly
Father, for she knows no other way.

Dad said it was time.
Mankind needed their Savior.
A promise is a promise
and Scripture must be fulfilled.

The Angel Gabriel appears
in her life so sweet.
Saying, "You are the chosen one
to conceive his son!"
"But how? she asks. "Like other women?"
"No, Mary, for the power of
God will come over you."

Your child will be without sin and will be
called the "Son of the Most High."
"Wonderful counselor, prince of peace,
Almighty God."
Jesus is his name,
and he will save people from their sins.
O come, Immanuel for God is with us.
Overwhelmed, my humble Mom says, "Here I
am. Let it be as you say,
for I am a servant of God."
With no one but Elizabeth to tell; Mom then
waits for Joseph's return.
Surprise! What's this? Mom's belly swells full.
Bitterly weeping,
Joseph thinks she has been unfaithful.

He cries out,
"Who set this trap and did this evil?"
"I did not protect this virgin in my home."
"Family and friends will stone her to death."
"Should I hide her, expose her,
or send her away?"

Restless sleep and dreams come to Joe.
"Do not fear," the angel says.
God is with her and will protect you both.
You are entrusted with God's Son.

Judgment by our Priests comes next.
Mom and Joe drink God's wrath
to see what happens.
No harm to them so all accept.
They go home to know God's Plan.

Dad said it was time.
Mankind needed their Savior.
A promise is a promise
and Scripture must be fulfilled.

Hear ye, hear ye, all must be counted.
Hi ho, hi ho, off to Bethlehem we go.
It's almost time for me to arrive.
Labor pains are close; Joe searches for help.

No room at the inn, we settle for a small cave
with animals and straw.
Joe diligently finds a midwife to help
my Mom with my birth.
"Is she your wife?"
"No, we are still betrothed," he says.
This unnamed midwife is filled with
compassion and curiosity
for the quiet strength my Mom shows.

"It's a boy!" she says,
but Mom and Joe already knew that.
A bright, shining star illuminates the sky for
lowly shepherds to see.
Come one, come all! See God's miracle!
The focus is on my virtuous Mom and me as
my Stepdad shadows and
protects our every move.

Wise men, kings, or
just plain readers of stars;
These men and women came from faraway
lands with gifts of Frankincense,
gold and myrrh.
They knew a good thing when they saw it!
Warned in dream, they escape evil Herod.

Once Mom is purified and ready, my parents
present me at the Temple in Jerusalem.

No anonymity here!
Simeon and Anna exult me loudly.
Simeon replaced Zachariah and now God's
promise to Simeon is fulfilled.
He sees the Messiah and is ready to die.

Anna, too, gives praises out loud.
Look and rejoice! Look and rejoice!
"The promised child" is here!
Loving Mom listens and
ponders these things in her heart.
Many things were said earlier
with Elizabeth and now.

Dad said it was time.
Mankind needed their Savior.
A promise is a promise
and Scripture must be fulfilled.

Oh Herod, monstrous and mean,
Sent soldiers to murder baby boys
whom he thinks might be king.
One step ahead of him,
Joe is warned in another dream.
Off to Egypt we go until Herod is dead.

Beautiful, gentle Mama taught me the
scriptures, right from wrong,
and fed and clothed me.

She kissed my scrapes and "owies,"
gave me warm, gentle hugs,
and sweet kisses for the face of God.

Protected and nourished me
as I grew to manhood.
Always proud of me,
filled with patience and encouraging words.
Her goodness and joy shine through
as she worships our Father.

As we returned from Egypt,
we made our home in Nazareth.
My Mom never complains, knowing our
Heavenly Father always has a plan.
Her strength, stamina and self-discipline
set her above all women.
It's time for our long overdue
pilgrimage to Jerusalem.

Already 12 years of age,
"I must be about my Father's business."
Still so young, my Mom reflects on these
words, trusting in my Father in Heaven.
Oftentimes in the background,
but I am forever prominent in her life.
She believes in me!
A Mother's love has no boundaries.

She watched my ministry at a distance,
but I am always in her thoughts.
She confidently tells the servants in Cana,
"Do whatever he tells you."
My Mom: So kind as she continually thinks of
others, knowing I can do extraordinary things.
Always patiently watching and praying,
Watching and praying.

Dad said it was time.
Mankind needed their Savior.
A promise is a promise
and Scripture must be fulfilled.

The words that pierce her heart come true.
This Mother of mine, so strong and brave.
She shows all others
how to trust and believe,
Even though my death and torture ravage her
simple convictions in life.
She is with me every step of the way.
Never abandoning me. Never forsaking me.
Her emotions are ripped apart as she
witnesses the agony of my crucifixion.
She's there…watching courageously through
suppressed tears. Not hysterically wailing.

"It is finished, dear woman, here is your son."
She is the beacon in the night.

A strong and steady light for others
to come and follow me.
Strength, compassion,
and grace encompass her.

In her life, she was sympathetic to others.
Aware of the embarrassment and
humiliation of her virgin birth.
She did not retreat from
my Father's Plan for her.
But she followed her heart
that was filled with peace and love.

The Holy Spirit was speaking and guiding her
With special gifts of compassion and love
for others and me.
Even before I was born, the Holy Spirit
entered her entire being
to make her who she was.
My Mom. I love you.

Dad said it was time.
Mankind needed their Savior.
A promise is a promise
and Scripture was fulfilled.

Butner Correctional Institution
Jerry Schur

You can meet some interesting people in a Federal Correctional Institution like Butner. I spent 36 months, less time off for good behavior, in that minimum security facility, as an unwilling guest of the Bureau of Prisons. It gave me time to study the frailties of the human psyche, a subject which has been my life-long pursuit. Greed, suspicion, ambition, egotism, hopefulness, you can see them all there.

My "co-vacationers" included a former Congressman, as well as a Chicago Police Commander, numerous businessmen, bankers, and overly creative accountants, not to mention some fund managers who were extremely successful it seemed, but only until their bookkeeping was scrutinized. Even Bernard Madoff was there. I didn't associate with him for fear he would sell me a bridge to Brooklyn.

One of the men I found interesting was Elmer Hunter, No. 3245-8946, six foot one, with a halo of blond hair that could have adorned a model. We worked together as clerk typists for forty cents an hour, a generous payment considering that the alternative was sweating in the laundry or cleaning toilets. Hunter and I were in the same dormitory, and we commiserated with each other over the frequent prisoner counts, the mandatory lights out and get-out-of- bed times, and the assembly-line meals when we had been accustomed to five-star restaurants (and huge tips).

When we first talked at our typists' desks, Hunter proclaimed his innocence. I had read the newspapers about him but remained silent. He asked me what I was in for and I replied, "financial crimes." Apparently, he had never read about my minor exploits in the tabloids, but he respected my privacy and never inquired further. I told him of my intentions to get released from Butner, recover my secret cache of money and get lost in France in the Dordogne.

Later, as we worked, ate and slept on the same schedule, he opened up. With an obvious pride in his accomplishments, he related how he had met a rich widow, pursued her and persuaded her to elope. Since elopement did not allow time for a prenup, he thought he was set for life, but he discovered that all her wealth was tied up in a trust, not just tied up but locked up beyond his reach. After a few years of what is often called marital bliss, he sought surcease of boredom in other boudoirs. She paid him handsomely for the divorce and he squirreled away millions beyond the reach of any authority.

In addition to that, his wife in happier days had secured for him a position as vice president in her family's business. His undoing was to embezzle a small king's ransom which he later told the government he had squandered on crap tables, slow horses and fast women. The FBI didn't believe him, but they couldn't find the money.

So, he ended up in Butner, wifeless, jobless, but far from penniless.

Another man I studied was Thomas the Assessor. That was how he introduced himself. The Assessor had a round, bald head and a body round as a beach ball. He bragged about his wealth and how he had run his Louisiana parish, unchecked until the FBI bugged his office. He pleaded guilty to taking three hundred thousand in unrecorded gifts from builders seeking his favorable attention. However, in the luxurious confines of Butner, he confided to me that his actual enrichment was many times that. He showed no contrition and vowed to run for office again as soon as he was out. He felt his people in the parish were a forgiving people, and he would be re-elected. Only this time he'd have his office swept for bugs every day.

He planned to collect enough money to live comfortably and then disappear, leaving his wife. "She was my high school sweetheart," he said, "but I'm out of high school now." Then he would go to South America. "It's easy to get lost there," he said. "Even Sherlock Holmes won't be able to find me." I liked his lack of pretense. What you saw was what you got.

As the time for my release neared, I opened up to Hunter. Sitting at our typewriters, I told him his friendship had helped me get through some dark days. I told him I wanted to tell him about myself, things I had never told anyone, and he promised to keep our conversation secret. I asked him, "Did you ever hear of LIBOR?"

"Yeah," he said, frowning. "It's something about London interest rates."

"Let me tell you," I replied. "Once a day a consortium of international banks sets a benchmark of interest rates for borrowing periods ranging from overnight to one year. They announce these daily at 11:00 AM. Now how much money do you think a guy could make if he knew in advance what the Libor rates would be?"

"I don't know. You tell me."

"These rates are relied on all over the world. Mortgages, bank loans, credit card rates are all affected by LIBOR. I'm talking trillions of dollars. A few hours of advance notice could make a homeless bum into a diamond mine owner, if he knew what to do."

"And you knew what to do?"

"I tried it on a small scale before I came here. It worked."

"Yeah, but the key is getting that information in advance. I bet it's all in computers with high security."

I leaned closer to him, though there was no one within ear shot. "Of course, it's all computers, but there always has to be a human in there and humans have weaknesses. I spent a month in London with some local private detectives. I found the right human." He just stared at me so I went on, "This guy will get me the information, not for overnight rates, they're too short. Six months or a year. Those rates are volatile and that presents opportunity. I've set up my organization, one broker in New York, one in Dallas and one in San Francisco. I get the data from London. I send a securely coded email to each of my brokers with their instructions. They buy or sell the right securities in moderate quantities. I don't try to get rich overnight. Too dangerous. Moderate transactions are ignored, and I wait a month or so between moves. In two years after I'm out of here, I'll stop, but I'll have more wealth than an Arab prince."

"That kind of operation takes money," Hunter said. "If you're trading futures or bonds you have to have working capital."

"Of course, but that's all set up. I have three investors. Each puts up a million. They are on board. I pay my man in London, and the brokers in the US get their commissions plus a nice bonus under the table. I split the balance with my three investors, and everyone is smiling."

Now Hunter paused while he was considering. "Do you think I could get in on this? At least for a little?"

"Sorry. No can do. I have three investors. They are rich and willing. The set-up is perfect now. I've just been telling you this because you're my closest friend here. Let's try to get together after we both get out."

"Are you sure? Couldn't you make me a partner? Won't you reconsider?"

"Sorry, I can't. Business is business. Business and friendship are separate worlds, like a wife and a mistress. Two worlds that must not intersect."

He was peeved for a few weeks, but we had been thrown together in a strange, enclosed world. We couldn't avoid each other.

Then about two weeks before I was due to be released, I pulled him aside. "Look, Hunter, I've had some bad news. One of my investors backed out. I can work the deal with only two million, but three is better. If you want in, let me know. I need a million bucks now. Yes or no."

*   *   *

I've been out now for about two years. Living in Argentina is good. I'm learning Spanish. I live in a small town with all the luxuries that money can buy, which is all the luxuries there are.

I don't know how long it took Hunter and Thomas the Assessor to get together and figure out what happened. A friend told me that they had tried to follow their money transfers to me, but that got them nowhere. They probably looked for me in France, but they'll never find me even if they look here in South America. The local police chief is a close friend of mine. We drink Gancia and play chess every Tuesday.

If they had studied human nature as I have, they would have known who was vulnerable and who could fleece the vulnerable. Maybe then they would have looked to find out why I was in Butner. If they had Googled me they'd have found the newspapers preceding my trial which often referred to me as the greatest Ohio con man of the last fifty years.

Palm
Cheryl Silverman

Looking up at palm
Looking back at me today
Makes my body calm

Forgiveness – Part 1

Denise Conner

I believe that we are, all of us, at the beginning of our lives, victims of our circumstances. If we allow ourselves, we can stay victims for our entire lives.

When we are so focused on being victims (and many times this is not a conscious choice), the focus is inward, on us, on what others have done to us, and our perspective of how people treat us is...as a victim. Others may not even be persecuting us, but through our victim lens, it tends to be what we see.

It is scary and exhilarating to realize we truly have power...and sometimes that change is too scary, and we don't take that chance to save ourselves. We go back to what we know, what has become comfortable to us; because we've chastised ourselves too many times to believe that we can change. And so maybe...we miss that opportunity to change. But life offers many doors, and it is never too late to change yourself.

Never.

We do have to be careful though. The only true way to change ourselves is for ourselves, not for anybody else. If we don't truly want the change, if it doesn't resonate within our souls, we will be lying to ourselves, and to others, and the change simply won't happen.

The first step—the most important step—is to stop seeing ourselves as victims.

How do we do that? If I've been abused by people I trusted, how do I stop being abused? And even more importantly, how do I keep myself from becoming an abuser? I believe this step begins in forgiveness.

For ourselves.

We can think about forgiving others later—that's a different story.

My ex was a victim. He would never admit it or realize it, because he was also a narcissistic bully. But he wore his victimhood like a cloak; he would brush it off and bring it out whenever needed. It was his reason for verbally attacking me whenever I was upset by his behavior and told him about it, as me being upset was somehow an attack against him. I thought that if I could just love him enough, if I could just show him real unconditional love, it would heal him. I thought that staying would protect his daughter. It didn't.

Almost nothing I said to him, or showed him, about giving unconditional love, ever took.

I now believe staying made it worse for her, because in staying, I normalized and enabled awful behavior.

He couldn't hear anyone else's pain. He couldn't recognize that he was victimizing his own family because his own suffering was too loud.

I had given all my power away when I married him, and I didn't know how to change it. I didn't know it was there all along, giving me chances, showing me doors. My strength had been hidden from me, as I think it is for all of us who have experienced childhood trauma. I was a victim then as a child, inappropriate sexual touching from a trusted babysitter. When I tried to be a savior for my ex by marrying him and became a stepmom to his then seven-year-old daughter, I turned into a victim again. I got lost; it took me many years to find myself.

So, my ex was a victim who turned into an abuser, and I was a victim who re-victimized myself.

How did I beat victimhood?

—By taking that first step.

—By truly forgiving myself.

—By taking responsibility for my actions and mine alone.

—By listening with the ears of a survivor, beginning to hear the truth, to notice the doors, to open them.

—By leaving the situation I was in, I learned how to love myself, and others, fully. I've been rewarded with the most beautiful life—more lovely than I could ever imagine.

I Wonder Why I Wonder Why I Wonder Why / Sex and Violins

Phil Silverman

I Wonder Why I Wonder Why I Wonder Why

Said a young woman
thinking about getting old
I wonder why I wonder why
I dream of silver and gold

A young man by himself in a crowd
Thought out loud
Who are these people and
do I need to be told?

They say:
"I wonder why I wonder why I wonder"
And the more they wonder
What it's all about
And the deeper they go - the more shallow

Was The Incredible Shrinking Man's greatest
fear his smallness?
That he would be infinitesimal?

Said an old woman thinking
about being young:
"I wonder why I wonder why…
with so much time gone"

An old man singing to himself in a park
Singing out loud

"Who cares that I forgot the
intro of the song?"

They say:
"I wonder why I wonder why I wonder"
And the more they wonder
What it's all about
And look through a telescope lens
They can't know the beginning from the end

Sex and Violins

I like to dance to the cha cha cha
I love that syncopated beat
I like to talk hot to a slow fox trot
And a Charleston is good for the feet
But when it comes to good old loving
A symphony
Won't do it for me
"Roll over, Beethoven"
and let in Jerry Lee.

She shouted
"Uh-uh-uh-uh!
Baby-baby-baby!
Shake me up, country boy!
Hold me tight, no fuss and fight!
Let's rock in the jailhouse tonight!"

Bug

S. Ramagopal

He thought the fifth word was bus
But when he saw the stranger,
he asked, buk?
You just missed the buck, she said.
The creating god was still thinking
That familiarity is a magpie
That tarnished the gut-fire.
What? Buk? He repeated.
Buck! The deer, dear! She woke him up.
The jogger with the arched-spine
was turning back early.
It's everywhere, he said, unsurprised.
Oh, it was crossing the playground!
Oh, yeah?
The vine with profuse blossoms
with the crimson corolla had made
no cucumbers but two browning pods.

From Cookie to Dollar Bill Excerpt
Fred Cantor

I come from a sports family. My grandfather was on the ESPN series, SportsCentury. My dad caught a championship-winning touchdown pass at Ohio State. My brother Marc, who is four years older than I am, overlapped with Julius Erving at the University of Massachusetts, and their coach loved the way my brother played the game; in fact, Marc, along with Dr. J, was named to the All-Yankee Conference Team.*

That's not a typo at the very end of the paragraph above. You know how you frequently see a tiny asterisk alongside a bunch of claims in an advertisement for a car lease or a credit card? Well, I worked in consumer protection law for many years and, as someone who firmly believes in full disclosure, I think it's necessary to give you some background about my family so you can get a sense of my roots as a die-hard Knicks fan.

And, unlike many of those car lease and credit card ads, I'm not going to bury the real story in small print. I'm going to give it to you straight—up front—right now.

My grandfather was, indeed, on ESPN's SportsCentury. His picture flashed on the screen during a documentary about Rocky Graziano which was still a very cool experience for me. I mean, how many people get to watch ESPN and then get to exclaim: "There's Papa!" He was in the photo because he had some connection to Rocky—exactly what, my mom is not sure. And I never asked Papa or my dad while they were alive what that connection was. What I can tell you is this: my grandfather is depicted on the cover of the paperback edition of Graziano's autobiography, *Somebody Up There Likes Me*. He arranged for my mom and dad to visit Rocky's training camp -- where Rocky and my dad posed for a photo "duking it out" over my mom who was standing between them. Last, but not least, my grandfather lost a bundle on the third Graziano-Zale fight. My mom still has vivid memories of a shoebox filled with cash that my grandfather lost that night on a bet.

My grandfather was a passionate sports fan who also went to lots of baseball games at both Yankee Stadium and the Polo Grounds way back in the day. That's something else I neglected to ask him, how on earth did he go to so many games when they were only played during the daytime way back then? Didn't he have a regular job to go to every day? All I can say for sure about that is when I was very young, Papa gave my brother and me an autographed baseball signed by a bunch of players on the 1932 New York Yankees including Babe Ruth, Lou Gehrig, Bill Dickey, and Lefty Gomez. Baseball memorabilia was not a thriving market in the early 1960s, so we didn't give any thought to trying to preserve those autographs. In fact, Marc and I even tossed the ball around from time to time.

The final factoid you should probably know about my grandfather, his nickname was Cookie. Come on, admit it, how many of you have, or had, a grandfather with the nickname of Cookie? That's got to be a rare thing, right? And doesn't that sound like the nickname of a diehard sports fan?

My dad clearly got at least some of his passion for sports from his father. Back in the early 1960s, when the New York Giants were perennial NFL title contenders, my dad had season tickets at Yankee Stadium and he would take me to one game a year. With stars such as Charlie Conerly, Y.A. Tittle, Frank Gifford, Rosey Grier, Sam Huff, and Erich Barnes, I was always psyched to see the Giants play in person.

My dad played softball on a regular basis back then. One of my two earliest childhood friends, Steve, recently commented on Facebook in connection with a photo of my father, "I still can remember your dad showing me a huge bruise he got sliding into a base playing softball. I must have been about 10. It made such an impression on me that I can remember it from 58 years ago, but now I sometimes can't remember why I'm standing in front of the refrigerator." I remember that bruise as well; in reality, it was a giant, very painful-looking raspberry. And, at that time, my dad frequently played on asphalt softball fields in area schoolyard playgrounds, so I wince at trying to picture how that slide took place.

Another close childhood friend, Big Al, remembers how, when I was in high school, we would have two TVs lined up side by side in our den (and occasionally even three!) so that my family could watch multiple games at once.

Incidentally, my mom was an avid sports fan, too, even though she grew up at a time when girls really weren't given much of an opportunity to play sports. As an adult, she was active in local bowling leagues into her 40s. And, if she had been an assistant coach under Pat Riley, I'm convinced Patrick Ewing would have won an NBA title. (More on that later.)

As for my dad's championship touchdown reception at Ohio State: he was only 5'6", so that TD was not on behalf of the varsity football team under legendary head coach Paul Brown. Instead, it was in a fraternity/intramural title game. I learned about this from one of my father's frat brothers long after my dad's death, so I never did hear anything first-hand from my dad about that moment of glory.

As for my brother, Marc, and Dr. J, they did indeed both make All-Yankee Conference and they absolutely played for the same coach in the same year; but they didn't do it on the same team or in the same sport for that matter. And no, I have not lost my mind. Marc's varsity soccer coach at UMass was also the freshman basketball coach at a time when freshmen were ineligible to play varsity sports; and this was during a time when coaches at the college level were given the responsibility for coaching more than one sport. So, yes, Marc and Dr. J both had the same coach. And, thanks to Marc and Coach Broaca, I heard about Julius Erving long before he became a household name.

Happy 97th Birthday to My Love

Sunshine Lutey

Soon after we met,
at the beginning of our journey
You introduced something new
that helped to shape our destiny.
You said we'll share many adventures;
you were so very adept as you told me all
about a most exciting concept.

It was an expansion in the
world of imagination
that you shared
during our conversation.
"Honey, let's take a ride on my
magic carpet.
We can go anywhere;
there is no limit."
Since then we've had many adventures
-- some imaginary, some actual.

I can list some very
important ones that are
actually factual.
We traveled to Cancun,
Mexico and to many states by
plane or car for games, for
fun, for special holidays – we
traveled near and far.

We formed a group and then produced 24 musical events; loaded them to YouTube; gave

proceeds to charity ($110,000) – every cent.

In 2015 we extracted 30 songs from shows beginning from the first show in 2008 through 2014 and created an album -- the "Sunshine and Raindrop Sing" album, which we shared with family and YouTube; but will it will bring us stardom – perhaps not.

In June 2019 we experienced our most treasured dream. Just us on stage plus a piano player, Jackie O'Neill, we sang for 90 minutes. It was an

accomplishment supreme.

But let's return to the
imaginary, we can do, and
we can go anywhere --
As we carefully step onto
our magic carpet and
gracefully float
into the air.

Maury and Paul
Jack Mullen

"Are you nuts?"

When there was no answer, Morris (Maury) Roth said it again. *"Are you nuts, Paul?"*

"I'm just begging for one more, Maury."

Roth turned and spoke to the empty chair at their table in Restaurant 19. "He comes three thousand miles to tell me he wants to do one more job."

"I came three thousand miles to *visit* you," Paul Zelinski said.

Roth talked to the chair again. "To visit me! He hasn't seen me since we retired twenty years ago. Now we're eighty-nine years old...he wants to do another job. Oy Vey!" He clutched his martini. "The man needs serious help."

Orthodox Jew, Morris Roth, and Roman Catholic, Paul Zelinski, had met for the first time on the hospital ship, U.S.S. Haven, as it steamed from Korea to San Francisco with its wounded cargo. Both had been soldiers in the 25th Infantry division of the 8th Army and both had been wounded on the same day while fighting in Operation Ripper---the fourth battle of Seoul.

A mortar blast had torn Zelinski's head open, while Roth had suffered leg and chest injuries from automatic rifle fire. After treatment and discharge, both had returned to their homes - Roth to the Brownsville section of Brooklyn and Zelinski to Quincy, Massachusetts, across the Neponset River from Boston's skyline where he welded hull plates at a shipyard.

Crime drove Roth out of Brooklyn. He told his friends, "If God lived in Brownsville, he'd get mugged." Zelinski found his friend a clerical job at the shipyard and Roth settled into a nearby apartment. Neither ever married.

In 1986, the shipyard shut down and the two men, surviving on disability checks, became business partners.

Roth had moved to Laguna Woods Village in 2000 when they shut down their fourteen-year-old operation. Zelinski stayed in Quincy and, though they hadn't seen each other, they talked on the telephone once a week. Neither had anything to do with texting or email.

Zelinski got out of his chair and stretched. He was a lot taller than Roth. He looked out over the patio railing at the tall, healthy trees. "It's a golf course in the middle of a beautiful park," he said. The word park sounded like "*pack*." When he sat again, he took a long pull on his beer.

"So, Maury, am I going to meet this new girlfriend? Is it Esther? Or Gloria?"

"Gloria passed."

"She's the one who lived with her daughter."

"No, that's Esther. You won't see her. She's in the hospital. Getting a new hip."

"Is she the one with the great keister?"

"That was Harriett. Harriett used to say, 'A man without a woman is a bachelor. A woman without a man is a genius.'"

"What happened to her?"

"She got the Alzheimer's."

"But this Esther, a new hip? What they can do these days, huh?"

"I wish they could give me a new schlong."

Zelinski laughed. "Your action days with the girls are slowing down, Maury."

"I had an Uncle Aaron. When he was an old guy and we were having a drink I said, 'Uncle Aaron, I got a question.' Then I asked him what you asked me. He laughed and said, 'I used to get around pretty good, Nephew. Now all I do is buzz and buzz and talk about what a helluva fella I wuz.'" Roth pointed at himself. "Now I'm Uncle Aaron."

They both laughed.

"You ready to order?" Roth said.

"Nah. I got no appetite anymore. You go ahead."

Roth settled for crab fritters and tomato basil soup, then thought again about Zelinski wanting to pull another job, leaned closer to the table and said softly, "Tell me, Paul. How come we never got caught?"

"We were lucky."

"Yeah, luck's the main reason, but why else?"

"We switched M.O. You'd go in one time, me the next."

"What else?" Roth said.

"We had...what do you call it? Chuter..shutter...?"

"Chutzpah. But Chutzpah had nothing to do with not being caught. What else?"

"Only you and I ever knew," Zelinski said.

"You and I and your priest," Roth said.

"The hell with my priest. Only you and I."

"You never confessed?"

"*Maury,*" He took a long swallow of beer. "I gave up my religion when I shot that North Korean in the face and found a picture of his wife and kids. That boy was no better or worse than me or you. He was there shooting people because his country told him to."

Anxious to move on, Roth said, "Why else didn't we get caught, Paul?"

Zelinski polished off his beer. "We never hit in Boston. Hell, we never even hit in Massachusetts."

"Right! I didn't want to be standing next to some putz in the grocery store who looks me over and says, 'Hey, you stuck up my restaurant!' Roth reached for a fritter. "I still say you're losing your mind, Paul.

****

The next day Roth gave his friend a tour of the village.

"Beautiful, Maury. And all these security gates."

"Keeps bums like you out of the property. How about we talk to a realtor? Even a schmuck like you would make friends here."

They drove back to the condo and talked some more.

"So...this therapist. You never told me about that," Roth said.

"Who goes around admitting they're going to a shrink?"

"Tell me that diagnosis again."

"With the fancy name -- *Anhedania*. It's an inability to experience pleasure. They say I'm socially withdrawing."

"You have been for years."

"I got trouble sleeping. And I eat like a bird. You know how I *used* to eat."

Roth decided to throw it out there. "How much of this depression is about Lee Remick?" He saw Zelinski stiffen.

Zelinski stared at the floor for a long time.

"Her father ran Remicks's Department Store in Quincy and he hired me to sweep floors. His kid would pop in from time to time, a pretty little thing."

"You told me once you dated her," Roth said.

"It would be a stretch to call it dating. My old man played cards with Mr. Remick, so I got to know him and the family. He and his wife divorced, and Lee went to New York with her mother; she was about fifteen, home visiting her father, when I was on leave, just before Korea. So, I asked her out."

"You went out with Lee Remick?"

"Yeah. Just the one time. See, she was fifteen. I was nineteen. Her father said, 'Okay, but an afternoon movie.' We saw *Annie Get Your Gun* with Betty Hutton."

"Did you kiss her?"

"Are you kidding? Didn't even hold hands." Zelinski looked across the living room. "If that girl had kissed me, I would have gone A.W.O.L. and never got shot and never known you and never…."

"You called me the night she died," Roth said.

"July 2, 1991."

"The cancer," Roth said.

"The cancer."

Zelinski stared at the ceiling. "It wasn't right, Maury. She was just a kid."

"Do you know you've called me every July 2nd since?"

Zelinski said nothing.

"Have you told your therapist about her?" Roth said.

"Of course not. There's some goddamn things you don't talk about to strangers." He wiped his brow with his fingertips. "I wanted to kill that guy who raped her in *Anatomy of a Murder*."

"Jimmy Stewart?"

"No, no, no. Jimmy was the good guy."

"Jesus, Paul—"

"And Jack Lemmon. He made her a drunk in *Days of Wine and Roses*. I wrote the son of a bitch a nasty letter, but he never wrote back."

****

In mid-afternoon, they drove the seven miles to Laguna Beach and sat on Roth's favorite bench watching joggers and cyclists and girls in halter tops.

"I got the guilt," Roth said. "I love my life, Paul, but you don't like yours."

They watched a volleyball game start up on the sand. "You don't want to live, Paul. You even quit taking your meds. One day I'll get a call, my friend. Paul did a swan dive off the Hancock building."

"Prudential Tower. It's taller."

After Roth put his arm around him, Zelinski said,

"I been depressed a long time, Maury. But you know what? When we were in business together, I was a happy guy. When we'd hop in the car and drive to New Haven or Bar Harbor or Manchester or wherever, it was *exciting*. I'd be looking forward to it.

Then, after pulling the job, driving the fifty or a hundred miles or whatever back to Quincy, I'd be alive. *Happy!"* Zelinski pivoted, faced Roth. "I want to do it again. Let's do it one more time, Maury." He grabbed Roth's arm. "It'll make me better. I'll get happy. Just one more time. I promise."

"Jesus, Paul."

"Remember the restaurant job in Greenwich - where we lucked into the big poker game in the manager's office?"

Roth remembered. They had driven eighty miles that evening to the wealthy village on Connecticut's Gold Coast where New York City hedge fund managers and investors lived and partied. Zelinski had been the inside man that night and had stuffed ninety grand into his pillowcase. The morning after they were safely back in Quincy, the Greenwich Times newspaper announced that a friendly Pinochle game had been victimized by an armed bandit. The players turned out to be a dentist, new car dealer, contractor, veterinarian, and Wall Street trader.

It had been their biggest score. Second biggest was from a huge supermarket in Providence. But mostly they hit high-end restaurants at closing and every penny of prize money went directly into Vanguard mutual funds. They had carefully averaged about five holdups a year for fourteen years.

The Laguna Beach surf was calm so disgruntled surfers were floating on their boards. A stray Frisbee bounced onto Zelinski's lap and a tattooed girl with green hair scrambled to retrieve it. A few minutes later they struggled to their feet and headed for the car, Roth using two canes.

****

That evening an exasperated Roth said, "So what are you thinking, Paul?"

"Something simple and quick. Maybe a donut shop."

"A donut shop!" Roth slapped his forehead. "This is a stickup. Gimme me all your crème-filled." He stared at his old friend.

"Paul, we were brave soldiers. Then we became crooks. Stuck guns in people's faces."

"*Unloaded* guns."

"But they didn't know that. We cheated people out of money they'd worked for. We were bad guys. Now you want to be a criminal again. Risk everything?"

****

The night before the job they sat in Roth's kitchen and mapped it out. Talked about what might go wrong. After Roth lit up a king-sized cigar on his patio, they hatched the plan.

"And remember," Roth said when they'd finished, "Just before we leave for the job tomorrow night, we pour whiskey down our Shirt fronts."

****

When the time came, Zelinski sat behind the wheel of Roth's car half a block from a small shop with hats in the window. *Chapellerie*. The store was empty except for a young girl doodling behind the counter.

Zelinski was shocked when two men in suits and ties led Roth out of the store in handcuffs. Arms waving, Zelinski jumped out of the car, struggled to keep his balance and yelled, "Hey, take me, too. I'm with him. He's my buddy."

The detectives were startled and the tall one drew his gun from a shoulder holster. "Freeze," he shouted.

"It's all my fault," Zelinski shouted back. "You don't need to handcuff him. He had a cap pistol!"

After handcuffing Zelinski the cops piled both of them in the back seat of the detective's car. The short cop was behind the wheel. The detectives began rifling through the two wallets.

"These dipshits are eighty-nine years old," the tall detective said.

"Both Korean War vets?" the other one said.

"YOU GOT THAT RIGHT," Roth yelled.

"Were you in the same outfit?"

"Yeah, but we didn't know each other till we were on the same hospital ship. Meeting this schlemiel was a terrible day. Worse than the day they put a metal plate in my head."

The tall one turned in his seat. "What outfit were you two in?"

"25th Infantry, 8th Army," Zelinski said.

"25th Infantry? Hell, my grandfather was 25th Infantry in Korea."

"What was his name?" Zelinski said.

"Higgins. Homer Higgins. Did you guys know him?"

"Ah...sounds familiar. A tall guy like you?" Zelinski said.

"That's him!"

"I forget where he was from." Zelinski said it slowly.

"He was a Texan."

"Is he still alive?"

"He passed last year."

Zelinski sat upright. "That's right. He *was* older. We called him Pappy. He was the bravest soldier I ever saw. In one battle, he stood up with bullets flying all around him and shouted, 'Come on, you dog-face soldiers. Take that goddam hill.' Then Pappy Higgins started singing *The Eyes of Texas Are Upon You.* So up the hill we went. May Pappy rest in peace."

The tall detective swiped at a tear running down his cheek. Looked at his partner. "We can't book these guys."

"Can't book 'em. What are you talking about?"

"For Chrissakes. They're war heroes. And they smell like a barroom floor. He had a toy gun. All he asked for was ten bucks. This was a lark."

"It's risky, Frank. What about the girl?"

"I'll go talk to her. Take her temperature."

****

Their robbery victim, a petite blonde in a pants suit, was laying the phone down.

"Have you talked to anybody yet?" the detective asked.

"I'm trying to call the owner. Keep getting a busy."

"Okay. Let me tell you about this guy. It's quite a story."

****

When the tall detective got back in the car, he took a deep breath.

"She's okay with it. Said when he let go of one of his canes to open the jacket and show her his gun, he nearly fell. When he said he only wanted ten dollars, she felt sorry for him."

"Hey. How come you guys were in there waiting?" Roth said.

"We've been getting eaten up by two guys pulling jobs in Laguna Hills and Mission Viejo. So we put teams on stakeout."

"We were looking for a couple of professionals, not Frick and Frack," the detective behind the wheel said.

After the cops walked them back to Roth's car and left, Roth stared at his partner. They were both trembling.

"Did you really know this Pappy Higgins guy?" Roth said.

"Hell, no. Never heard of him."

"You always were a better liar than me."

"At least mine was a little lie. I didn't tell them I had a plate in my head."

Roth rolled his eyes. "So…what's next, Paul? I suppose tomorrow you wanna go stick up Disneyland?"

Zelinski laughed. "Naw. We're retired. I'm flying home tomorrow. Let's go get a steak. I'm buying."

Saying Hello to the Cello
Dennis Glauber

When Mstislav Rostropovich passed away in 2007 a month after his 80th birthday, he had long been hailed as the greatest of all cellists. One tribute from a fellow cellist claimed, "He has done more for the cello than any musician has ever done for any instrument." Indeed, he gave the world premieres of well over a hundred compositions. I am among the many millions who respected him enormously, but I had no reason to believe that we would ever meet or that our eventual brief encounter would make this reminiscence worth reporting.

Evette and I usually shun invitations to "meet the artist" receptions. They are overcrowded and the artist frequently looks as though she/he would rather be anywhere else but there, fielding fatuous questions after an exhausting evening's work...on an empty stomach yet. But back in December 1998 we were intrigued to receive a written invitation to a sit-down dinner in the Founders Room at Benaroya Hall following the evening's concert given by the Seattle Symphony with Rostropovich as soloist.

Although we had been generous donors to the Symphony within our limits, by no stretch of the imagination could we be regarded as major benefactors, and to this day we have no idea why we were included. We accepted, of course, and I knew that in the very remote possibility that we actually got to speak to the great man, I already had a topic of conversation in mind.

We had good friends in San Francisco named Sue and Felix Warburg. Felix's father Gerald had been a cellist of professional quality who had his own string quartet and actually owned all four of the instruments, all Strads. After his death, his cello had come into the possession of Rostropovich, and Felix had told me that he was determined to go backstage after his San Francisco concert scheduled two days after the concert in Seattle. So, what a conversation opener I had up my sleeve!

We could hardly believe our good fortune when we gathered in the Founders Room to find that the intimate party was for just 40 people at four tables, and wonder of wonders, we were at the honored guest's table with only the Music Director seated between me and Rostropovich. When the toasts had been drunk and the applause had died down our conversation went something like this:

Me: Maestro, I have a friend in San....

He: Not Maestro, you call me Slava.

Me: Thank you, Slava; I have this friend in San Francisco, a man of our age….

He: What do you mean our age, a young fellow like you?

Me: Slava, I know exactly when you were born, and I'm six weeks older than you. My friend is the son of Gerald Warburg.

He: Gerry Warburg! A wonderful man. I have his cello. We must drink to him (rising and giving me a great bear hug). And tell your friend he must come and see me after the concert.

For the rest of the evening, the conversation focused on his wife, Galina Vishnevskaya, the famous soprano who had remained at home in Paris, severely crippled by rheumatoid arthritis. This was the very week that the FDA had given much publicized approval to the new and promising drug, Embrel, for the treatment of rheumatoid arthritis. Slava was anxious to get hold of the drug immediately. He and his young manager were leaving the next morning for concerts in

Portland and then San Francisco. I told them that by pure coincidence, we too, were going to Portland the next day, not for his concert but to spend the weekend with our physician son and his family. By the end of the evening my mission was clear.....try by any means to get hold of as much of the new medication as possible (never mind the cost, whispered one of the zillionaires to me) and deliver it next day in Portland. The manager and I exchanged phone numbers, and Slava graciously signed our program, putting in his own quirkish stamp by Russifying Evette's name to Evettchka.

From then on, events moved quickly. Early Friday morning, I called my friend, David, whose company manufactured the drug, only to learn from his wife that he was in a meeting In Philadelphia ......a blank. A call to my former hospital -- yes, it was on the formulary but not yet available......another blank. A call to my son in Portland -- his hospital didn't even have it on the formulary......blank blank blank. A call from David in Philadelphia giving me the contact who might be able to help. Said contact unavailable......blankety blank.

By midafternoon, we were on our way to Portland and on arrival, at about 6:30 pm, there was a further message to call Slava's hotel. When I reported my lack of success, the manager graciously offered me two free tickets to the concert. I politely declined but said I would accept four tickets, and then without bothering with dinner, our daughter-in-law with an excited 12-year-old grandson in tow, made what should have been a 30 minute drive in 20 minutes. We took our grand circle seats with seconds to spare. Slava was, of course, wonderful in a program different from the previous evening's offering in Seattle.

Slava had given me his Paris address in case the medication became available later, but I decided not to pursue my chase. I did not feel it was my place to procure a drug about which I knew nothing (oral or injection? refrigerated or not? to be reconstituted or not? side effects?) to be used by a Paris doctor who would know even less. So there ends the mini saga of Slava and me with just a postscript that the following evening in San Francisco, my friend Felix was indeed able to say hello to his father's cello!

My Babies, My Promise:
The Journey of My Soul;
The Louise Sullivan Story

Foreword: Nancy Brown

In February 2020, I came into possession of a 580-page typewritten story authored by Nanny, my great-grandmother, over 100 years ago and tucked away for many years, unknown to most in my family. With the Coronavirus pandemic just beginning, I found myself under a stay-at-home order with lots of time to read this document. Her stories pulled me into the life of a remarkable woman with an insatiable drive to serve. This was a story that needed to be told.

Nanny was an amazing woman with a heart filled with love...love for 168 babies whom she fed, clothed, bathed and "mothered" throughout a 13-year period from 1915-1928. She never took one cent for any of her "baby work," but felt directed by God to care for her babies, dedicating her baby nursery to the memory of her biological son, Kenzie, who died from diphtheria at age 17. After nurturing unwanted babies in her community, she paired them with permanent families, initially in homes in Chicago, IL and subsequently in Pasadena, CA. In reading Nanny's story, I experienced a deep connection to my great-grandmother who passed away when I was just eight years old. Through my own faith, I felt compelled to tell Nanny's story to the world, just as she would have wanted.

I immediately partnered with a cousin who shared my fascination with Nanny's life. We connected with two adult children from the last babies Nanny raised. The four of us became determined to make Nanny's dream come true. Additionally, three of Nanny's grandchildren, two of whom are in their 90's, gave insight into Nanny's life through their own personal experiences. While simple editing was within our capabilities, organizing this story from her stream-of-consciousness format into a readable book became a daunting task. We are incredibly grateful to our outstanding editor who helped us tell Nanny's story in a concise, cohesive manner. We are also appreciative to our many family members and friends for their generous donations in making Nanny's journey become a reality.

This story is more than a treasure for our family legacy. It is our desire to dedicate this book to those who selflessly care for, foster, and adopt the unwanted children of this world. It is a story all will want to read...a story of how one woman's faith and devotion can make a difference in the life of a child.

When to Talk?

Peg Zuber

They picked me up off the street.
Brought me here. Locked me up.
They wanted me to talk…
I'm not going to talk. Why should I?

I don't know why they picked me up.
I might have been staggering…a little.
They said I had no friends or ID.
No ID?   I'm not talking.

This lock-up is strange, many females;
many scratched and smelly.
Stay away from me.
Whew! I'm not talking.

Hey, look! Someone is getting out?
When will I get out?
Maybe I should speak up?

A Uniform is coming toward me…
Better speak up.
M-e-o-w.

I Kinda Did
Sunshine Lutey

It was May 2021; I was vaccinated, my extended family was vaccinated, and I was flying to Las Vegas to see my children and their families. The last time I was with them was September 2019 when I shared a trip to San Diego with some of them. Soon after that, the pandemic started; I hadn't seen my family in over 18 months.

David wasn't up to traveling, but he had a wonderful treat because his daughter, Alison, traveled from New Orleans for a surprise visit. David went to a restaurant for the first time since March 2020. She arrived the day before I left and stayed until I returned.

I spent three wonderful days with my family. Some of the family hiked at Mount Charleston.

The final day was reserved to spend time with my son, Darrell; but some medical appointments delayed us. Suddenly, there I was alone with little Saoirse, my two-month-old great granddaughter. I'm not exactly a baby person; in fact, tiny babies scare me.

But there I was, holding Saoirse. It wasn't too bad; she wasn't crying. I began to sing to her. But then a horrible odor filled the air. I carefully got up and gently laid Saoirse in her bassinet and took care of business; I got the diaper on backwards but hey, who would know?

I'd been warned that she would fuss if her diaper was wet. Sure enough, she soon began to fuss. This time I grabbed a new diaper and carefully looked; aha, there were the tabs. I decided to open them ahead of time. *Whoops, I pulled the tab right off and it won't stick back on*; I got another one. I'd been warned, "Place the new diaper under her; she likes to pee when the diaper is off." Well, it was mostly under her, but not well enough. The bassinet sheet was soaked, her romper was soaked. I fastened a clean diaper on successfully. I noticed her romper had a large neck; I slipped the romper down past her shoulder, body, and pulled it off her legs; then I grabbed a clean one. I looked at the romper; I looked at Saoirse; *well, the neck is pretty big*. I decided to put it on over her feet first so I wouldn't have to put it over her head. I got it over one tiny foot, but she was kicking wildly, and I couldn't get it over both feet.

Imagine my relief as Denise opened the door and walked in; I handed her the romper. She scrunched the whole thing up and slid it over Saoirse's head with the greatest of ease.

When all the appointments were done, we left for Darrell's home where my talent with babies finally shone as I took picture after picture as Saoirse smiled
.

I smiled, too, as I told my family, "I took care of Saoirse – well, I kinda did."

Scenes from a Clubhouse Pool
Phil Silverman

(Loud indistinct arguing coming from stage right into spotlight)

Guy #1: I saw you comin'! I saw you comin'! You were lookin' at me!

Guy #2: Damn right, I was! You're not supposed to smoke that close to the gate!

Guy #1: Go to hell!

Guy #2: I'm already *in* hell smellin' your breath!

(Beautiful woman arrives from stage left, wearing a robe over a bathing suit; men stop arguing and look directly at her; long-haired brunette removes robe and bends down to lay a blanket on the recliner. Then lies face down on the chair and moves hips right to left to get comfortable).

Guy #1: (Starts to speak, nothing comes out).

Guy #2: ......(pause) I'm tellin' ya!

(Security guy arrives on the scene, from stage left).

Security Guy: Ok, guys, what's going on? (Opens up small notepad).

Guy #2: This guy told me to go to hell!

Guy #1: I was just giving him directions!

Security Guy: Ok…what? What's the issue here?

Guy #2: This guy lights up a cigarette about two feet from the sign over there not to smoke within the… what do ya call?

Guy #1: Pure speculation.

(Woman gets up from the chair and starts to apply liquid sunscreen to her body. All three men freeze).

Guy #2: (pause) I know what I saw. Look, all I saw is smoke over by the fountain, or whatever.

Guy #1: Well, I hate to surprise you, but I would not blow smoke on them nice fishes!

(Woman laughs, as she applies a lot of sunscreen to her legs).

Guy #1: Ya see, even she agrees with me! I am pro-environment!

Guy #2: You may be "pro" but you're sure not mental!

(Woman laughs again). Woman: You guys are so funny!

Security Guy: (Shaking his head, looking up at the sky): Can we move along? Is there a problem here? I don't see one. Look, sir, (to Guy #1): Please smoke within the designated area. (to Guy #2): You can chill out, heh? (Woman stands up to comb long hair).

Guy #1: Care for a smoke?

(All three guys step forward toward the woman).

CLOSE.

Zooming through the World

Ellyn Maybe

Gratitude to the events happening around the
world on *Zoom*.
Listening to readings, lectures and concerts
from all over the sphere is a wondrous thing.
The logistics of turning on the computer and
being in a library in Brooklyn,
a museum in Portugal,
a concert in Scandinavia.
All is possible.
Walking into *Zoom* is like a world
encapsulated amidst this hum of time
in an askew Dali universe.
Melting clocks.
Van Gogh sky.
Stars lifting their ears to whisper at us
like a seashell understanding how the world
has become tiny like a thimble
and large as an ocean eternity.
Simultaneously seeking events
and connection with all the
ancient and new solitude.
Blending in a dance.
Learning new steps.
Twirling through the hemisphere.
The future wearing invisible ink.
Unclear and profound.

Forgiveness – Part 2
Denise Conner

I had an epiphany the other day, while I was driving.

I firmly believe that forgiveness makes me stronger. If I can forgive my ex for stealing my retirement, then I truly will have peace in my heart.

And now it's time for a mini-rant about the evils of losing your retirement during a divorce. (Grab a few kernels of popcorn.)

I've always believed that going after your spouse's retirement in a divorce is evil.

Yes, back when women stayed home, gave up their career dreams to take care of the kids while men made all the money, and divorces meant the mom and kids were destitute while the dad went to Tahiti (or wherever, just someplace else, away from any regrets)—back then, the divorce laws regarding retirement at least seemed to make sense.

But in this day and age, when both men and women work, it is ridiculous.

Whoever makes the most money in a divorce (if they've been married for a magic number of years—in some states it is 10, others more or less) must legally give part of their retirement to the other party, unless they give up a huge asset (if they even have it, like a house, for example).

This, in my opinion, is evil, and benefits slackers, no matter the gender of the recipient. The recipients feel the retirement portion is their property and chuckle their way to the bank as if they hit the monthly lottery.

It truly is not their property, no matter what the law says. They did not work the spouse's job.

Yes, they might have done other things in the marriage, but I firmly believe that retirement should be off the table in any divorce.

I have been divorced twice previously, twice before this, and I never even considered going after my spouse's retirement.

OK rant over. Breathe in, breathe out.

Now, my forgiveness epiphany: My ex had a pretty horrible childhood, at least according to his own personal story. He was the middle child of three, and when the kids would get in trouble and line up for belt whippings (for stupid stuff), he would be in the middle and get twice the number. He was verbally abused as well. He didn't remember until about halfway through our marriage that it was his mom who was the worst. (Red

Flag: If the male partner can't stand his mom and refuses to truthfully work through the issues, chances of a successful relationship are zero to nil.)

Now there's a legal connection between us that will only go away when one of us dies. Every month, he gets a check, a nice grand, from my retirement. And every month, when I have allowed myself to think about it, I've gotten angry all over again. I've never sincerely wished for someone's demise before (no, not even the prior POTUS), but this one, truly, has been hard for me. I've prevented myself from that sincere wish by imagining how sad his daughter would be if she was to lose him, and that's helped me to avoid any ill-wishing.

Yes, wishing is very different from acting. But the problem with wishing is this: The evil wolf that lives inside us all grows stronger with ill wishes.

So, what is my epiphany? How do I feed my good wolf, and starve my evil wolf?

Maybe, I'll change my perspective. That monthly retirement deduction feeds my karma; it also detracts from his karma. It wouldn't detract if he used it to help his daughter, but he doesn't. I know this because of things she's told me.

With my new perspective, I no longer get angry every month.

Never Too Late
Nancy Brown

Guess I'm a late bloomer. Growing up with no interest, experience, or skill in any type of sport, something clicked when I turned 28. Maybe it was the intrigue of a new tennis club less than a half mile from my home that led me there. Or perhaps the need for some common interest in my marriage that knew little. Maybe it was the desire to introduce our children to a sport that looked fun. Who knew it would end up being such a huge part of my life from then on?

What started out for the adults as a $5 all-you-can-eat-and-drink Burger & Beer Rallies, turned into so much more. Junior Team Tennis at the club, high school tennis and junior USTA tournaments for both our son and daughter, continued to six months of coaching tennis in Australia for Mark and one season of college tennis for Nicki. For me, the sport included playing USTA Leagues, President of the Junior Tennis Patrons at the Club, and USTA Jr. Satellite Chairman, and box seats one year at the U.S. Open Tennis Championships in New York. But there was more. I became U.S. Director for my own business, Worldwide Sports Exchange, and traveled around the world leading groups of junior tennis players to live with families, play competitive tennis and experience the culture of the countries we visited, including playing on artificial grass in New Zealand and even real grass in Australia. Friendships blossomed between adults as well as teenagers, both local and international. Even a resurrected marriage emerged. To say tennis became a huge part of my life is an understatement.

Fast forward to 1994 when, after 28 years of a now failed marriage, I decided to "run away from California" and life as I had known it for 48 years. I didn't take much with me...28 boxes of clothes, a few knick-knacks and, of course, my tennis racket where I landed in Alaska, the Last Frontier, for the next eleven years. It was a bold move, for sure, but I felt more peace in that journey than I had felt in years. It was here that I learned that tennis could also be played indoors. In fact, that's where it's mostly played. After all, it snows from October to May in Alaska!

After retiring from teaching in Alaska, I moved to Illinois where my daughter was now married with two children. Being a "long distance grandma" just wasn't working for me. What to do in Illinois, now that I retired from teaching? Well...teach again. Of course, I continued to play tennis, making many lifelong friends in the process. It was there that I heard about a new sport: pickleball. In the community where I lived, friends would play tennis at 8 AM on Saturday, followed by pickleball at 10:30 am. That progressed to several days a week, all year long. Indoors in the winter and outdoors in the summer, I began to love pickleball more than tennis, finding it to be a great form of aerobic exercise and so much easier on my body. Pickleball had taken over. After ten years in Illinois, I moved back to California, concluding that I didn't want to be shoveling snow when I was 80. My arthritic body rebelled, and two years of surgeries followed...a shoulder replacement on my "ball toss" arm, arthroscopic knee surgery following a skiing accident, and a total hip replacement the following year. My post-surgery goal was *always* to get back on the courts...the pickleball courts.

I learned that it was never too late to have an evolutionary season...from tennis to pickleball. I am enjoying a little friendly competition, whether it be a game, a tournament, a ladder, or the Laguna Woods Village Games. Having played tennis just once in five years and feeling pain in my "good" shoulder, I decided that pickleball was better on my body, to say nothing of the comradery I now experience with over 300 of my closest friends! While I don't know where I will go from here, I hope to play pickleball well into my 80's and even beyond, as many of the seniors here in "the 'hood" do. Never a dull moment, for sure!

An Age Problem
Marcia C. Hackett

Today I was subjected to a blatant case of age discrimination. A representative of a local animal placement service told me quite bluntly that, due to my age, she was not allowing me to foster and/or adopt a beautiful, young male cat.

I've been an animal lover and pet owner all my life, having grown up with beagles. As an adult I've owned four Dalmatians, a large cockatoo, and six cats. Three of the dogs and all six cats were rescues. Three of the latter were obtained from the same agency that denied me this time! Animals have always been an integral part of my life.

I heard about the approximately three-year-old male rescue, available for adoption, from a friend. My current six-year-old female Olivia, obtained two years ago, is a small, beautiful Russian Blue with a heavy fur coat and green eyes. She's loveable and cuddles next to me on the couch when I read, or in bed when I sleep. I've been looking for a male pal for her. When I heard about the rescue, I immediately called and answered many questions regarding my experience with cats. The placement staffer and I made arrangements for me to visit the cat to see if I really wanted him. The last question asked of me on the phone was my age which I answered truthfully, having no reason to lie. I'm an active, healthy, high-energy woman, one who plays tennis four or five times each week, am enrolled in three college classes, do volunteer work for several organizations, and on and on. In other words, I don't sit around watching TV. Age is only a number to me; it rarely affects how I live my life. And I take very good care of my pets. A sign on the wall in two of my rooms says, "I love my pets." So true.

The staffer and I met on a Friday afternoon at the first foster's home. The cat immediately came to me, let me play with it, and hold it on my lap. I thought the fit was a perfect match, that we could bond easily. I explained again that I wanted to foster first to see if the male and Olivia could get along. If so, I intended to adopt. My home is safe, with an indoor atrium where my animal loves to sleep and sun herself. Olivia's also free to roam the house, sleep on several beds, and use the scratch trees.

As I left the home that Friday, I handed the officer the required paperwork. She practically assured me I could have the cat. She would call the next day or Sunday to set up a time to deliver the animal. Delivery would likely be Sunday or Monday, two open days for me. I returned home, excited to be bringing a new pet into my life. Then, nothing happened for six days! I couldn't understand why.

Finally, Thursday morning I got a call from the same adoption agency staffer; she said quite abruptly that "due to my age" (which, of course, she had known from the start), her organization would not allow me to foster or adopt the cat. Stunned, while questioning her, she denied saying that she'd promised me the cat, that she'd heard me indicate I wanted it and planned to foster first to see if the male got along with my female; if so, I would adopt. I was so offended, angry and flabbergasted I hung up the phone. *What should I do now*? *Fight the decision*? This woman knew nothing about my lifestyle or ability to care for pets. Furthermore, certainly no public organization would include in its bylaws an age limit regarding adopting a pet. *How could the agency get away with these criteria*, I wondered? In defense of her decision the staffer had repeated the approximate age of the cat (2-3 years), intimating that he would far outlive me. Of course, I understood that. None of us knows how long we'll live. Wouldn't it have been more considerate of my age and feelings to simply say other folks were interested in the cat, and the agency had decided to give it to one of them?

I considered writing a letter to the editor of our local newspaper but what would that accomplish? This was a clear case of age discrimination, illegal in the workplace but perhaps not in the pet adoption business. Also, coincidentally, May is known as "Older Americans Month," presumably to honor seniors and all they contribute to our society. Ageism definitely still exists.

Because the discriminatory interaction with the placement staffer bothered me a great deal, seriously affecting my psyche regarding my age and ability, I contacted the president of the agency. I was polite, giving her my side of the story. She listened carefully, apologizing for her associate's behavior, and indicating the agency's best wish was to place an animal in a good situation *only once*, hoping the owner outlived the cat. Although the staffer either didn't know or failed to inform me, the new policy is *not* to place a cat, especially a young one, in a home with another cat. Had the associate told me that, I also would have understood.

The president and I parted amicably with her telling me she would have a "long discussion" with her staffer.

It's a known fact that multitudes of animals are waiting in shelters to be adopted by loving, new owners. I pledge to keep looking for the "right one" to join Olivia and me. At the same time, I'm saddened about the cat I almost got, but hopeful that the right home is found for him, too.

Korean Delight
S. Ramagopal

Two petites, baseball caps,
sun visors, squat, and busily
Forage, like voracious locusts,
some blooming leafy weed
Blanketing the stream's bank
and stuff into large paper bags;
Seen them, in the same area,
two days in a row.
I approach, watch for a while,
when, the one in a navy-blue petticoat
Perhaps sensing my shadow,
raises her head and says, Hi!
Wondering if she was fluent in language,
What are these? I ask her.
Right away she goes, "This is good!
Very good for herbal tea, see
How it smells!
Yes, yes. People ask us, curious!"
She is on a roll:
Where are you from, you're tall!
Yes, some Koreans are tall, some short
this grows all over on
The mountains in Korea;
we dry them to make tea...
When I ask what they call it,
she turns to her friend in a
Pink petticoat to exchange

as though my inquiry was hilarious.
Shuk! Shuk! both say, and kept laughing...
and keep foraging
Delighted in discovering the cornucopia...
Centuries ago, they say,
a Korean Prince fell in love
With a handsome Tamil Princess
and married her.
I clip a piece of the plant
and crush it and bring it closer to my nostrils,
as they continue...
Hanuman, avows to resurrect Lakshman,
his Lord Rama's brother
Is on the sky to the Sanjivani Hills, and,
below
In the island shores of the epic battlefield.
Shuk! calls out Ravana, his FBI General,
Wait! I'll go myself there
To the demon, Kalanemi,
and cut that monkey game!
And now
Where's the Korean Delight?

Charlie in Syria - 2

Alan Dale Dickinson

Charlie's dear old friend, Jan Smoker, CIA Director at the Agency, called him just as soon as she heard that he got back to his beloved LA (Los Angeles}.

She wanted to know why Charlie faked his own death, then went to one of the most dangerous places on the planet (Syria), and what the heck happened while he was there.

She was extremely happy that our man Charlie was not dead, but alive and still kicking. Also, she admonished him never to do such a stupid and life-threating thing like that ever again.

Then Charlie told her that he would never have survived his ordeal 'in-country' had it not been for his C-Team (Charlie's Team - - Peggy, Sarge, and Sundee).

He recanted to Jan just how each of them had saved his 'bacon,' so to speak, on several occasions on his little excursion into the face of Death!

Charlie started off by telling her one of his favorite and very old Irish sayings/poems, being an Irish laddie. Charlie loved old Irish sayings and he also loved St. Paddy's Day. The poem that he quoted read like this:

"May the sun always shine
on your windowpane;
May a rainbow be certain to follow each rain;
May the hand of a *friend* always
be near to you,
And, may the Lord fill your heart
with gladness to cheer you on!"

Syrian President *Bashar Hafez al-Assad's* Army was ruthless as well as quite brutal. They used poison gas on the FSA Freedom fighters, had President Putin's Russian newest jet fighters continually strafe and shoot up the rebels (as they called us), as we tried to free some of the captive northern Syrian towns.

Charlie also told Jan that none of the world's other free countries would help the Freedom fighters because they were afraid of Russia. Also, if any of them interfered with President Assad's *genocide* of these innocent, honest and good people, whose only crime was that they wanted a little bit of freedom from his oppression and constant harassment, they would die.

Sundee, Charlie said, found him pinned down by a sniper in Aleppo's Bell tower. Every time he moved the sniper almost took his head off!

Finally, the sniper caught him trying to get to a safer place behind a thick wall, and then all of a sudden, the sniper put a bullet through his right arm. Bam. Bam. He told Jan that it felt like a red-hot poker.

Luckily for Charlie, it was just a through and through GSW (gunshot wound), and he barely felt it or so he says now. Two more shots just missed his handsome face.

Then out of nowhere, literally nowhere, Sundee somehow had climbed up the tower, and managed to sneak up behind the Syrian sniper, and took him down in seconds and tied him up. She did not take him out as she knew that the FSA would want to question him.

Peggy, Charlie also told Jan, saved his life when he stepped on an IED (Improvised Explosive Device); it blew him about 10 feet in the air. Luckily, he said, he landed on a pile of soft sand, so he only got minor scrapes and bruises. Then Peggy dragged him to safety before the deadly sniper could put a bullet in his brain.

The IEDs, he told Jan, were invented by the Rebels in Sri Lanka, a small island off the coast of India, about 50 years ago during a major civil unrest.

Their IEDs were very crude, home-made pipe bombs, but they were extremely effective. The dreaded, murderous, and despicable ISIS (Islamic State of Iraq and the Levant) is still using them today in both Afghanistan and Iraq with very deadly results.

Sarge also came in very handy as Charlie had forgotten to bring his gas mask, and when the vile Syrian Army sprayed poison gas all over the town, Sarge appeared from the shadows, and gave him one.

The names of some of the very brave, and absolutely fearless Freedom Fighters that Charlie and his team fought with were: Commander Riad al-Assad (Assad is a very common name in Syria), Cornel Qassem Saad al-Din, Lieutenant Mararet al-Nuran, and Sargent Khan Shekihoun.

The Commander was an expert with demolitions and explosives. The Colonel was a logistics and weapons expert, and Lieutenant al-Nuran was a mine removal expert.

The three towns in Northern Syria that Charlie, his C-Team and the FSA, helped free and drive Assad's army out of them were named: Aleppo, Idlib, and Hama.

She Can Hardly Get Around

Phil Silverman

She can hardly get around
I can't pity her
I can only pity me
Because
she is what I will be!

I see a little old man
He can hardly get around
He won't wash his hands
after taking a ...
he's exactly what I will be!

If I'm LUCKY!

Lab Monkey
Jon Perkins

As happens occasionally when searching for a solution to a scientific problem, an error, a mistake, something outside the plan solves an entirely unexpected issue. So rather than an instance of human intelligence shining brightly in the morning sun, conquering forces seemingly beyond control, the proverbial monkey sitting in front of a typewriter writes the great American novel.

Henry V. (for Victor) Wellingham, a graduate student at ASU, mixing chemicals in a retort, was not paying attention, his eyes focused instead on the rear end of another student, Mary C. (for Chaste) Wilson. It being Sunday, only the two of them occupied the large chemistry / physics laboratory. Precariously close to the due date for project submission, each attempted to complete their over-ambitious assignment. Being dissimilar in almost every respect, Henry and Mary were not friends. And while Henry harbored unattainable thoughts of interaction with Mary, she was happily engaged in a partnership with another fellow. Thin, eyes the color of the ocean in motion, hair the color of sunlit sand, with a pretty heart-shaped face, Mary was a popular Pi Phi.

Henry, a doleful dweeb with a mop of mousy hair that hung on his shoulder, had few friends.

The burner beneath Henry's glass was on high, emitting a blue flame approaching the violet range. The concoction began to boil. Wisps of a yellowish cloud of plasma began to rise above the rim.

Simultaneously, a large tome on advanced chemistry balancing precariously on a shelf above the burner inched its way to the edge, propelled by the vibration of the bubbles in the glass. At the moment when Old Vic had a mental picture of himself welded to Chase's butt, the book fell off the shelf and landed perfectly on top of the retort. Instantly, a flash of energy sent the young man to the floor.

"Hey!" Mary exclaimed, turning in annoyance to face Henry. "What the hell was that?"

Henry stood and quickly extinguished the burner. He was astonished to see the beaker intact, although the contents had escaped. Then, scratching his head in bewilderment, he answered Miss Wilson's anxious question with all the intellect he could summon.

"I don't know."

Mary rolled her eyes. "You're pretty stupid, Henry."

"Thanks," he said without the slightest hint of guile. He peered at the empty flask and at the book that had resettled itself atop the glass and continued to scratch his scalp. Mary walked the few steps from her station to his. They stared together at the book and the glass.

"I think I saw a flash," she said finally.

"Yeah, me, too."

"Whatever was in there, it let loose a bunch of energy."

"Yeah."

After continuing to stare at the flask, she said, "What was in there?"

"A bit of deuterium. Some lithium. In a saline base."

"Ah." More silence. After a bit, she clenched her eyes and asked in a small voice, "Cold fusion?"

"Hadn't thought about it; I was working on a new battery concept."

Silence enveloped them both for some minutes. She considered the odds of him having stumbled upon something as consequential as cold fusion. Her eyes ranged between him and the empty flask.

The Nobel Prize in Physics intruded upon her thoughts.

"Think you could recreate that?"

"I guess so."

She looked up at him then, letting her eyes take on a sweet quality that was not in her nature. "Hey!" she smiled. "What about you and me having a beer?"

It's a New Day
Sunshine Lutey

It's a New Day Story

Early in January, I noticed something; it appeared as if I'd lost my happy nature. When I was by myself, my face looked cross; I was frowning. I thought *I want my happy feeling back; I'm going to practice smiling. It might actually make me feel better.*

I need to explain this a bit better. When I had many tasks to complete, my focus was on how much I had to do. This made the tasks a heavy load. With my new focus, I smile and find joy in each little task I finish. This makes a big difference in my attitude.

I awoke one morning with a plan to get up at 8 AM. As I got out of bed, David said, "Please stay with me!"

I had things to do, but I crawled back into his arms. I snuggled and enjoyed precious minutes. Suddenly my mind was ringing with a lovely melody and words I've never heard before. I didn't want to lose the melody and words. "David, I have a new song and I need to write it down."

I climbed out of bed and collected paper and pen. I wrote the lyrics and tried to hum the tune; the basic idea was still intact. I wanted a song that would bring joy as we began our 2021 year; the song did just that. The lyrics had a line about being by the ocean shore.

The next morning, I drove to Laguna Beach, which is one of my favorite places. I was there in less than 15 minutes. This was my first time there in months. I walked down the stairs to the beach and found a rock where I sat to enjoy the sights and sounds. I love to watch the waves as they crash against the rocks and roll onto the beach. The sound is perfection. Eventually, I turned on my phone's video and sang the song. Then I listened. I had almost captured the tune that had filled my mind; however, the background accompaniment was the sound made by the waves. It made me smile.

The trip back took much longer with bumper-to-bumper traffic. When I arrived home, I sat at the piano and recorded background music that would support my voice. I subsequently sang it in a recorded *Zoom* session and uploaded it to my

"Sunshine Lutey YouTube Channel;" I have been singing the song ever since.

It's a New Day lyrics

It's a new day, a new year
Wonder what it will bring.
Yes, a new day, a new year
I have a new song to sing.

Perhaps I'll take a ride
Walk near the ocean shore
Get needed exercise
Let my spirit soar.

It's a new day, a new year
Wonder what it will bring.
Yes, a new day, a new year
I have a new song to sing.

Some stories I will find
Waiting to be told
In mind, I'm growing younger
Instead of growing old

It's a new day, a new year
Wonder what it will bring.
Yes, a new day, a new year
I have a new song to sing.

I'll lie beside my love,
Hold on so very tight
Enjoy each other every day
Oh yes! This feels so right

It's a new day, a new year
Wonder what it will bring.
Yes, a new day, a new year
I have a new song to sing.

I have a new song to sing

Tiny Gray Lizards
Cheryl Silverman

Tiny Gray Lizards
A workforce of their own
Hedgehogs are jealous

SPAM

Marcia C. Hackett

There are various varieties of the food product called "SPAM" that I love; I hate the many unsolicited internet messages also called "spam" or known as "junk mail."

SPAM, a trademarked Hormel Foods Corporation product, was introduced in 1937 to increase the sale of pork. Pork shoulder cuts were seemingly not popular at the time. The pre-cooked meat in squared cans was advertised as "the meat of a million uses." The product's many advantages of "affordability, accessibility, and extended shelf life" awarded SPAM wide popularity in WWII, known as "special Army meat." At the time, refrigerated food for soldiers in the field was often impossible; SPAM in its small, easily stored can, provided the solution. The product became a ubiquitous part of the soldier's diet, and was introduced into the native diets in Guam, Hawaii, Okinawa, and the Philippines. In the United Kingdom Prime Minister Margaret Thatcher referred to it as a "wartime delicacy." Even Nikita Khrushchev in the Soviet Union is known to have said, "Without SPAM we wouldn't have been able to feed our Army."

One can see the food product has a history. There is a museum in Austin, Minnesota, a town called "SPAM Town USA" where visitors can learn about SPAM and its development during the past 80 plus years. The Hormel Company advertises their invention as having "no preservatives, 100% natural and no artificial ingredients, and low sodium." Critics of SPAM originally called it "the poor man's meat" and claimed it contained a pig's snout, ears, and innards in its homogenous mass. How true these claims are remains a mystery. However, billions of cans have been sold worldwide with a wide variety of added ingredients for the enjoyment of individual tastes. In Hawaii, the product is sometimes referred to as "The Hawaiian Steak." Residents have the highest per capita consumption in the US. SPAM is often eaten daily by some locals. Hundreds of recipes for SPAM are available online. I, myself, enjoy the "original" variety of SPAM occasionally; it serves as a quick dinner meat or filling for lunchtime sandwiches.

The term "spam" with no capital letters dominated the internet and grew exponentially in the 1990s. It is defined from Wikipedia as "unsolicited, electronic messages called spam, bulk or junk email, text messages, internet postings," generally with the purpose of "commercial advertising, of non-commercial advertising, or commercial proselytizing or for any prohibited purpose." According to Wikipedia, it is believed the word "spam" first became popularized in a 1970 Monty Python television show. Two customers enter a fictionalized greasy café and try to order breakfast only to find almost every item on the menu includes "SPAM" which one customer doesn't like. Other patrons in the café start to chant the ditty, 'Spam, Spam, Spam, Spam ... Lovely Spam! Wonderful Spam!" The song in this sketch became popular, resulting in the term "spam" being used to define unsolicited electronic communications. It is important to point out that recipients *have not* granted permission for these messages to be sent to them.

Here's why I get upset daily as I sit down at my computer to read my emails. Without exaggeration, I receive at least 100 spam messages a day; I have no interest in 99% of them at all! Following are a few recent examples on the message line: Flabby arms; Obesity Cure; Car Shield (for insurance); Sex chat; Back pain; Fix Tinnitus; Tax resolution services; Restore vision; Huge tummy; Male enhancement solutions (someone thinks I'm a male); Date Hot Asian women; Dr. Seuss says Hi; Prostate solutions; The Casino Special; Portable WiFi; Fungus destroyer; Total personal loan; Retirement Survival; Walk-in Bathtub Shop; Bark Begone (presumably for my dog); Lose up to 39 Pounds; Defeat the Fascist 14; Libido fix; YOU WON; Medical marijuana; Acid reflux; Knee pain relief.

In spite of keeping my spam filters updated to protect my computer accounts, I continue to receive these unrequested messages which take time and energy to delete. Once I log onto my computer, is there any wonder why I quickly hit "delete all" always hoping I haven't missed an important email? The latter happened last year when a dear friend's son sent a mass mailing to many friends for his mom's 90th birthday celebration. His message went into spam. Much to my disappointment, I missed the message entirely and the party.

"Spamming" has become a verb meaning use of messaging systems to send unsolicited messages to large numbers of recipients. Sadly, folks get paid to do this!

While I cannot live without my computer, I wish someone would invent an easy solution to help feed the world with SPAM and get rid of the electronic spam!

Pixels of 50 New York
William Scott Galasso

In Queen's, red brick rows on postage
stamp lots flank Main St., with weeds,

car exhaust, factory smoke and sidewalk
stands of steamed Sabrett hotdogs, while

nearby in Maspeth, where the Navy Yard
stood, a terminal district of transit lies tucked

between boroughs, as Manhattan's skyline
dwarfs East River oil slicks, asphalt stench.

Maybe on Fridays a trip to Brooklyn
Patsy's Pizza (best in town) or

Coney Island's Nathan's where cigar
smoke marinates with saltwater taffy,

while girls in shorts flirt with boys in T-shirts
as cigarettes rakishly dangle from lips

and a brass ring hangs from the carousel
on doo-wop, sticky, hot summer nights.

Strange as it Seems
Phil Silverman

People have a change of heart,
strange as it seems.
People have pretense to art
And dash all their dreams
Just as the cosmos keeps moving on.
We pass the baton,
Strange as it seems.

People all fall in love,
Smile as it beams.
People fall in love;
Don't know what it means
But it feels so right
And day is night.
People fall in love,
strange as it seems.

The Itinerant
Nancy Brown

We first met when I came to live with Dabby and Boss, my grandmother and grandfather. Where the names came from, I have no clue. I used to sit by Boss' side for hours, mesmerized by the sound that you emitted when he played. When I turned five years old and Mom and Dad got our first house, Boss let you come home with me. What a gift that was!

We were great friends for decades. I took lessons until I was in the 8th grade and even got the Hollywood Bowl Award one year for the "Most Improved Student." That award got its name because the winner would receive two tickets to go to the Hollywood Bowl to hear Dorothy Kirsten, a "glamorous and gifted soprano whose mother was an organist and music teacher, her grandfather a conductor and her great-aunt also an opera singer." You moved from Dabby and Boss' house to my house on Mercury Lane in Pasadena, then on to Mariposa in Altadena where you stayed while I went away to college.

But you were lonely -- no one to sit beside you and play. Then I met my husband-to-be in college, an extraordinary musician who played in a rock band all through high school and college and even opened a club in Lake Tahoe with his band after college. He adopted you and brought you to our home after we got married where you lived for over thirty years. You hosted many parties in our home and the wear and tear began to show with water rings from party glasses and plants on the top of you.

With the passing of time, you and I spent less and less time together, usually only at Christmas when I brought out my Christmas carols and played. Over the years, another family member, my gifted daughter, grew to know you and love you, taking lessons of her own and bringing sweet melodies into our home once again. After graduation from college, she moved to Alaska and the music faded more and more.

As fate would have it, my marriage didn't last; however, my relationship with you did. After a brief visit to my daughter in Alaska, the most beautiful place I had ever seen, I moved to Anchorage five short months later, where I lived for the next eleven years. Soon after I arrived, you were shipped 3,441 miles from Fountain Valley, CA to join me in Anchorage, AK. In spite of the movers' struggle to bring you to my upstairs apartment, we were at last together again. What a joy to have you in my life once more. I had my beloved music and tried to resurrect our relationship; however, you really belonged to my daughter.

The final leg of your journey was to Chicago where you were originally born. I shipped you to be with my daughter so she could bring those blessed melodies to life again. Somewhere along your journey and all those miles, you developed a broken bridge. I developed a broken heart when my daughter shared the news with me that she had replaced you with a baby grand. I was devastated! I went to visit you in the warehouse where your signs of age were evident. Not only a broken bridge accompanied my broken heart, but also numerous watermarks from leaking potted plants and party glasses from many celebrations. All that remained now was a thick layer of dust.

Built in Chicago, moved to California, onward to Alaska, you ended life in your final resting place, Chicago. You truly had come full circle. It was time to say "goodbye" to my beloved piano.

Thanksgiving 2020
Sunshine Lutey

Thanksgiving has always been the day we celebrate with various members of my husband David's family. But ever since COVID hit, I wondered what could be possible for Thanksgiving 2020. Every weekend David's son, Roger, and Shosie, came by to check on us. Everyone wore masks and they would stay for just an hour. When COVID first appeared, I wondered, *what will Thanksgiving Day be like this year?* Early in November, Roger and Shosie told us that they would bring us the fixings for a Thanksgiving celebration. Shosie asked me, "Do you have a special tablecloth and napkins that you would like to use to set the table? If you give them to me, I'll wash and press them and bring them back when we bring the food."

David was excited; "Then you'll have Thanksgiving dinner with us?"

"No," Roger answered, "that wouldn't be safe. But we'll bring some turkey and lots of other good things."

Sunday morning we awoke knowing it would be a special day. As promised, Roger and Shosie brought the sliced turkey and lots more goodies. As David, Roger, and Shosie conversed, I had fun preparing the table.

As usual, Roger and Shosie only stayed an hour because they were worried about keeping us safe from COVID. After they left for their home, David and I sat at the fancily decorated table and enjoyed turkey, potatoes, gravy, stuffing, cranberry jell, chocolate turkeys, and a special treat -- cheesecake from the Cheesecake Factory for dessert. David was overwhelmed, almost teary-eyed. They also brought a split of champagne which David and I shared. What a day it was – Thanksgiving 2020.

Panoptic

S. Ramagopal

I was walking, no, no
Actually, I was jogging today
To refresh a forgotten art, and
Pausing, at part of the chore (it was) done
On the sprouting grass behind the fence
And lowering forward to grip my knees
For a moment of death, recoiled—
Across
GOD zoomed by!
My vacant mind startled
—what the heck...where am...this...what
G.O.D.
G period O period D period
White
Capital, and yes, there was
A period after each (both the letters and
periods), buoyant
Flanking in black (outside) and red (inside)
Wane
Guaranteed Overnight Delivery
In new guth, in god, in Gothic, in vain
In God We Trust
U period S period A period

A Dance Prescription

Denise Conner

One of the many benefits of enrolling my granddaughter into dance classes is that I found out about, and enrolled myself into, a weekly one-hour class for adults.

The very best part about that is that my daughter has been doing the class with me.

The second-best part? I am learning a few new dance moves. We learned jazz the first two weeks, ballet the next two, hip-hop the last two, and next will be tap.

Of course, there's not a lot of time, so we only get enough knowledge and moves to be slightly dangerous, but it's fun. It gets the heart, brain and body moving (which according to new research, helps reduce dementia-type disease); and it greatly increases positivity of self.

I love to dance, and I don't really care how crazy silly I look. My husband tells me he thinks I look sexy and that's all that matters to me. But there's always been a little part of me, deep inside, that judges me. A little voice that says, "Really? You're gonna do that? Don't you know how silly you look?"

And I would always have to acknowledge, "Yes, I do know, but I don't care!"

Crazy are the conversations that happen in our minds…at least in my mind.

I've discovered that with this class, I no longer hear the little voice.

The funny thing is, I'm dancing even sillier. Especially after the hip-hop class, my attempts to isolate certain parts of my body are quite hilarious. I know, because of the huge mirror that is covering the wall in front of us. But somehow, that doesn't stop me from trying the moves on the dance floor at the venues we visit. I know they are still hilarious because my husband laughed so hard he almost fell down; but he danced with me anyway. He's even tried a few of the moves. And the coolest thing is that a lady I never met before came up to me after one of my most hilarious "episodes", hugged me and told me I totally made her night.

Laughter is good for the soul…and (my) dancing is guaranteed to provide it!

Rituals
William Scott Galasso

An alarm clock sounds 6:30.
I grope for the shut-off button,

pry open eyes, *yawn, stretch,*
splash cold water on skin, then

pouring coffee, I test morning air
surveying sky; is it blue or pewter?

Does air smell of snow,
hint rain, promise heat?

Are the clouds works by Monet,
or sumi-e brushstrokes of cirrus?

Do I catch today's news, absorb its trials,
postpone what's inevitable, perusing instead

my I-Phone before trekking to job
or a hike in hills, the sea below me,

Or is this the day I make time my own
and like Kerouac pick a direction, or live

as children do making the story up as it
goes, without a thought of its ending.

Songs from a Trip to China
Dennis Glauber

In October 1996, we were part of a group of 14 who spent a month traveling through China by rail, bus, river boat and airplane. Our various experiences led me to compose new lyrics to some familiar tunes. The first of our several ghastly train rides provoked the following:

Pardon me boy
Is that the Xian- Chongqing choo-choo?
It takes hours twenty-nine
To reach the end of the line
You get to use the toilet
Just a hole in the floor
Mind the rat poison
As you slam the door
Dinner in the diner
Feel just like a pioneer
Like no sane American
Has ever done before

Our tour leader arrived with an upper respiratory infection which he generously shared with all of us, prompting this response:

Coughing and wheezing and
Choking and gasping
Snorting and sneezing and
Croaking and rasping
Trying to loosen the mucus that clings
These are a few of my least fav'rite things

Lots of sore tonsils
And lots of red noses
All sorts of medicines
In increasing doses
How to dispose of
The mucus that clings
These are surely my least fav'rite things

But it's not bronchitis
Or laryngitis
It could be worse
So we don't make a fuss
Cos' we're riding a bus
And not a hearse!
(Yes, the bus was alive with the sound of
mucus!)

Of course there was the inevitable what
could be labeled Mao's revenge, and so with
apologies to Bernstein's EAST SIDE STORY:

I feel s****y
O so s****y
I feel s****y and c****y, oy veh!
What a pity
What a pity it's ten times a day!

Our final train ride before we succeeded in our demand to fly from immaculate airports on immaculate planes elicited this continuation of the original train theme:

When we saw the train
The one that goes Changsha to Guilin
We couldn't restrain
A certain now familiar feeling
If there were paint
You can bet it would be peeling
If there were a fan
You can guess what hit the ceiling
But there's good news, there is good news
Remember it well
We no longer have to use
the railroad from Hell
Yes, that was our last night
On locomotive Hades
From now on we sleep tight
Like gentlemen and ladies

And now here is the moral
My advice could not be finer
Never choose to use choo-choos
When next you visit China
Refuse abuse—- don't use choo-choos
When next you visit China!

Children's Pilgrimage
Peggy P. Edwards

Why are the children running away?
Thousands are fleeing, leading the way.
Leaving their homes, leaving it all --
El Salvador, Honduras,
Guatemala, Central America.
Why do they walk
through the night and all day?
Coming our way and begging to stay?
Why are their parents letting them stray?
What is it their people are trying to say?
Climate change, drug wars,
greed and decay?
Wake up! There is no time to delay.
The reconnaissance is upon us this very day.
Ignore all the warnings and soon we will pay.
The children are crying, they're fleeing,
They're running away
but there's no place to stay.

Here's Looking at You, Kid

Jerry Schur

Some babes are like a wad of gum on the bottom of your shoe. You can't get rid of them. Ilsa was like that. I owned a bar a short walk from Notre Dame. It was around 1940 and her husband was a political prisoner. Lonely woman, hungry man – my perfect setup. Oh, I admit I may have led her on a bit. I'm no saint, but you'd think a married woman wouldn't be that naïve. It's surprising she was so trusting she didn't see how untrustworthy I was. She thought of us as Romeo and Juliet. To me, we were Don Juan and some parlor maid.

When her husband's party members came to take her to him, I should have just said, "So long, kid." Instead, I got romantic. I hugged her and said, "We'll always have Paris." Her eyes gushed enough tears to raise the level of the Seine.

Fifteen minutes later she was ancient history. The approaching German armies were scaring my customers, so I fled to Morocco. I opened a larger bar and life was good. There were a lot of refugees there, many of them women, some rich, some poor. I didn't discriminate. The poor women were desperate, seeking favors from a rich club owner. The rich ones were bored and therefore, willing. All of them hoped to get to the U.S. or at least South America.

Then like a sudden rainstorm on a sunny day, who should walk into my place? Ilsa. Of all the gin joints in all the towns in all the world, she walks into mine, hugging me and whispering about true romance. She and her husband were on the run. They heard about me, and she insisted they run here. Her plan was to dump him for permanent bliss in my arms. The last thing I wanted was permanent bliss with one woman. Maybe with three, but never one. She refused to leave me, and kept asking my piano player to "play it again, Sam." He, a sentimental fool, couldn't say no to her. The customers were sick of that song. It wasn't much of a tune, really.

Desperately, I did something I'd never done before. I went to her husband. Another sentimental fool; he loved her. She couldn't stand up to both of us. We pushed her to do her patriotic duty. When I was sure she was leaving, I got romantic again. "We'll always have Paris," I said. Her eyes streamed enough tears to water half the Sahara.

When she finally left, I was sorry for a few minutes, but I felt like I'd escaped the jaws of death or worse, a monotonous, monogamous relationship. For no reason, I asked Sam to play it again, just once.

Then my buddy, Police Captain Renault, came in. "I was shocked, shocked to hear your girlfriend left town," he said.

"Women have a short shelf life. I guess you know everything that happens around here."

"That's my job. So, what are you going to do for female entertainment?"

"I don't know. I'll look in my black book and review all the usual suspects."

"In examining recent visas, I found that a Romanian princess has come here."

"I hope she visits my joint."

"Oh, I'm sure she will. I told her everybody who visits Casablanca goes to Rick's. Of course, I'll look forward to your customary, generous contribution to my personal retirement fund."

I folded some bills and put them in his uniform pocket.

That night a brunette in a flashing diamond necklace traipsed in. I introduced myself. Her name was Caradja. She smiled, an invitation. I slid my arm around her waist and said, "I think this is the beginning of a beautiful friendship."

I'm writing this because some idiots in Hollywood want to make a movie about Ilsa and me. I bet they screw it up.

The Authors

Barbara Ashley
How You Can Tell Your Own Great Stories

Barbara has been writing since she was six years old, when she wrote plays for her toys and younger siblings to perform. Her books for young readers, writers and artists were inspired by the interests and experiences of her students and created during her career as an elementary teacher.

Published Works:

Amazon: Rebels & Spies? - Civil War Novel; *Warriors & Peacemakers* - Sequel to *Amazons, Rebels & Spies?*

Published by Childwrite -- Interactive Books for Young Readers Writers and Artists: *Once Upon a Dragon, If I Were a Monster, Look at Me! I'm on TV!, What If…Extraterrestrials Landed Near Your Home, Where Can I Hide?, What Could "It" Be?, My Mother Goose Menagerie, The 3 Bears and I, You Can Be a Civil War Spy!,* and *Be a Civil War Spy!* (Game for all Ages)

Nancy Brown
Black and Yellow
Foreword to My Babies, My Promise: The Journey of My Soul; The Louise Sullivan Story
Never Too Late
The Itinerant

Nancy was born and raised in Southern California, "escaped" to Alaska, then to Illinois for 21 years before retiring and returning to California. As a special education teacher for almost 40 years, Nancy co-taught high school English for several years. During the COVID pandemic, Nancy discovered her great-grandmother's memoir, *My Babies, My Promise: The Louise Sullivan Story,* and published it on June 22, 2021, now available on Amazon. As co-editor of the *Village Stories 2021*, Nancy is deeply grateful to the Publishing Club for inspiring her to publish her debut memoir, *Full Circle: The Journey of a Wandering Soul*, due out in 2022.

Fred Cantor
From Cookie to Dollar Bill

Fred is a retired attorney who has also worked on a variety of creative projects that have been the subject of articles in the *New York Daily News,* the *Boston Herald*, and the *Hartford Courant* among other media outlets. He co-created the award-winning film, *The High School That Rocked!* which was the only documentary short invited to screen at the 2018 Rock & Roll Hall of Fame Film Series. The selection here is an excerpt from the recently published, *FRED FROM FRESH MEADOWS: A Knicks Memoir* (The Strickland Press), which the *New York Post* praised: "Here is a delightful book that I can't recommend highly enough...Fred Cantor's stories ring like a trusted friend's from the neighboring barstool. It's about time the Knicks became a source for fun, terrific literature again."

Carol Kangas
No Picture/Bio *Some Things are Just Meant to Be*

Denise Conner
A Dance Prescription
Forgiveness -- Part 1
Forgiveness -- Part 2
Sobriety

Denise retired from the University of Nevada, Las Vegas. She is the daughter of resident Sunshine Lutey. She began golfing at the age of 10, when her dad, Lloyd Lutey, had visions of her and her brother becoming pro-golfers. They both became captains of their high school golf teams, and she came in second in state in her senior year. She followed her brother into the Army after graduating, and after serving honorably for four years, again followed him to work at the University of Nevada, Las Vegas, for 30 years. Both started in Human Resources; he left that department to become Director of Computing Services, while she stayed at HR for 14 years, and eventually became a university police sergeant. Now she is almost a full-time nanny to her granddaughters; she spends the rest of her time singing and dancing with her husband for the fun of it.

Beth Cornelius
Love: I Love the Way She Loves

Beth, retired, worked as an educator for 36 years. She now designs and creates educational programs and plans contests for people who desire to lose weight. Beth and her husband, Art, sing comforting songs and give inspirational messages to patients in nursing homes. They both work to stay healthy by walking, biking, and eating healthy. They hope that these actions will promote a long healthy life for both and give them time to fully experience the love they share and their joy of living.

Barbara DeMarco-Barrett
A Longing for Buzz

Barbara is the editor of *Palm Springs Noir,* just published by Akashic Books, for which she also wrote a story. Her stories and essays are in *Orange County Noir* (Akashic), *USA Noir: Best of the* Akashic *Noir Series*), *Rock and a Hard Place, Dark City Crime Mystery Magazine,* and *Inlandia*. Her articles appear in the *Authors Guild Bulletin, Los Angeles Times, Poets and Writers*, and *The Writer* magazine. She taught at the UC-Irvine Extension, where she received a Distinguished Instructors award, and is professor of creative writing at Saddleback

College's Emeritus Institute. Her first book, *Pen on Fire* (Harcourt, re-released by Mars Street Press), was a *Los Angeles Times* bestseller. She hosts *Writers on Writing*, KUCI-FM.

Alan Dale Dickinson
Charlie, the Private Eye in Syria
Charlie in Syria - 2

Alan is a native of the great state of California, making him one of the very few Native Sons. He was born in downtown L.A. (Los Angeles).

He wrote and published 20 mystery novellas which are published in 14 foreign countries around the Globe.

Dickinson retired as Vice President and Business Banking Manager of the World Corporate Lending Group, from Bank of America, which is the largest bank in the United States, and the thirteenth largest bank in the World.

Dickinson completed a Bachelor of Arts Degree in Business Administration-Finance with a concentration in accounting, economics, real estate, and management and holds a Lifetime Community College Teaching Credential from the State of California.

He once had a bank office on the 'Queen Mary' Ocean liner permanently docked in the lovely Long Beach Harbor.

Peggy P. Edwards
Children's Pilgrimage
Forest Gumpess
Mientes – You Lie

Born to a polyglot family in Mexico City, Mexico, Peggy's fascination has always been language.

She spent most of her career as a bilingual teacher and taught preschool through university. She also helped many immigrate through Amnesty. She retired and moved to our Village in 2004. In 2013, Peggy founded the Village Publishing Club and in 2015, the Club published the first *Village Stories*.

Peggy's second love is music. Her ukulele is essential to her wellbeing. She published *Alfabeto Crossover Alphabe*t and *Lalalandia*— eight bilingual stories in which music saves the world.

William Scott Galasso
Grace Notes
Gypsy Wind
Pixels of 50 New York
Rituals

William is the author of seventeen books of poetry including *Mixed Bag,* (A Travelogue in Four Forms), (2018); *Rough Cut: Thirty Years of Senryu* (2019); and *Legacy Thirty Years of Haiku* (2020) available on Amazon. He's been published in 250 journals, participated in 300 readings, and appeared on radio and TV programs in New York, Washington, New Mexico and California. He co-edited *Eclipse Moon*, the 20th Anniversary issue of SCHSG and serves as an editor for the *California Quarterly*. He's a member of *Who's Who in America.*

Dennis Glauber
Matters of Grave Concern
Saying Hello to the Cello
Songs from a Trip to China

Dennis Glauber's fine-chiseled stories have been included in our *Village Stories* from its inception. A retired anesthesiologist, he migrated from South Africa to America in 1980. He is a favorite storyteller at the Publishing Club's Storytelling in September. He is also published in *The Hummingbird Review* and in several journals. He was a prize winner in the

Village Library's writing contest. He also writes the program notes for the Community Concerts of Laguna Woods Village. He is a Shakespearian scholar.

Lorraine Gow
When They Cross the Border

Since emigrating from Honduras, Lorraine Gow has experienced America from a variety of unusual perspectives: a "black Latina" girl growing up in a black neighborhood, a black girl whose family is related to the Latinx community, and a black, Latina woman fully integrated into a middle-class, white environment. Her writing reflects an attempt to blend a matriarchal, Central American culture with America's Hispanic, black and white melting pot. Her theme has always been an immigrant woman's journey to find her way through this kaleidoscope called America. Ms. Gow authored *Black Women with Tamales* and recently contributed to *The Truth That Can't Be Told Anthology* (both available on Amazon). You can also find her writings in *Village Stories 15-20*, *Lummox Poetry 5*, and *Life and Legends Literary Journal*. She is currently working on a second collection of short stories and a children's book.

Contact Ms. Gow at – lorraine2writes@google.com

Marcia C. Hackett
SPAM
A Gift to Myself
An Age Problem

This is Marcia's second year as a contributor of stories to the Publishing Club 2021 Anthology. Her attempts at writing memoirs began about 10 years ago and resulted in a self-published book last year of personal and family stories. Now, she is concentrating on non-fiction essays and some travel memoirs while continuing to participate in Saddleback

Emeritus creative writing classes. As a world traveler, Marcia has enjoyed visiting many amazing places, and met people in five countries where she taught conversational English as a volunteer. Who knows? Maybe all these experiences may result in a second book of essays.

Sunshine Lutey
A Bit of Christmas
*   From the Gifts' Point of View*
Freezing – Roasting
Happy 97th Birthday to My Love
I Kinda Did
It's a New Day
Thanksgiving 2020

Sunshine always had a song to sing while growing up. After high school, she married Lloyd Lutey and moved to California. During 43 years of marriage, they raised two children. Sunshine enjoys her family, including her granddaughter / great granddaughters. Sunshine earned a BA degree in Psychology/Sociology from San Jose State University. She designed and programmed business systems. She lost Lloyd due to illness in 2005; she subsequently married David Hartman. Between 2008 and 2019, they produced two musical shows yearly. They scheduled four 2020 musical shows but canceled all of them when the pandemic hit. Sunshine continues to sing and play the piano, bass guitar, and electronic horn. She currently conducts multiple *Zoom* gatherings. Besides Sunshine's love of music, she enjoys writing. She published three autobiographical books (available on Amazon), which focus on her love of music, family, and life; she plans to keep writing.

Website: SunshineCharities.com
Email: SunshineLutey@gmail.com

Doug Sainsbury
The Walker

Douglas F. Sainsbury was born and raised in Chicago's west suburbs of Oak Park and River Forest. He attended and graduated from Oak Park-River Forest High School (Ernest Hemingway's alma mater), and then attended the University of Illinois graduating with a BA degree in English. Following college, Doug received a JD from Kent Law School.

Doug then spent a tour in the Army, including fourteen months in Vietnam. His paramount assignments were Legal Specialist and Public Information Officer (News Reporter and Photographer).

After military service, Doug worked in the consumer credit and banking industries, including nine years with the Federal Reserve Bank of Chicago.

Doug retired to Southern California in 2011 to be closer to his children and to pursue his lifelong dream of writing fiction. *Intrusion, Phantasm, and Emergence comprise the Jeremy Chambers series,* and *Trillions* is his forth novel. Doug can be contacted at dougsainsbury@gmail.com.

Jerry Schur
A wedding to Forget
Butner Correctional Institution
Here's Looking at You, Kid

Jerry graduated from the University of Wisconsin, Madison, after a detour in the U.S. Navy during World War II. He then spent three intellectually stimulating years at Yale Law School. After that, he practiced union-side labor law in Chicago for 48 years specializing in litigation, often before administrative agencies. When he retired, the firm had grown from two lawyers to 18. His hobbies are the Civil War, playing bridge and writing.

Ellyn Maybe
Fermata
Zooming through the World

Ellyn Maybe, Southern California based poet, United States Artist nominee 2012, is the author of numerous books and widely anthologized. She has a critically acclaimed album, *Rodeo for the Sheepish* (Hen House Studios). Her latest poetry/music project is called ellyn & robbie. Their album, *Skywriting with Glitter*, has also received high praise. She also has forthcoming collaborative poetry projects with Joshua Corwin including *Ghosts Sing into the World's Ear* (Ghost Accordion series 1st Wave, Mystic Boxing Commission). "Zooming through the World" was first published in the *Laguna Woods Globe*.

Jack Mullen
Maury and Paul

Jack Mullen was born in New York City and raised in Pasadena, California. After serving as a U.S. Marine in Korea he was an Eastman Kodak salesman before joining the San Diego police department. He worked patrol, vice, armed robbery, and homicide. After retiring, he wrote a police fiction novel, became agented, and sold the manuscript to Avon Books which published it and a second novel in the mid-nineties. He holds a Bachelor of Science degree from San Diego State University.

Other Publications
In the Line of Duty: Avon Books
Behind the Shield: Avon Books
Dear Jerome…Letters From a Cop:
Copworldpress

Jon Perkins
Fear and Greed
Hell's Bells
Lab Monkey

Jon Perkins is a retired executive now following his lifelong desire to write fiction. He has an MBA and a pilot's license, and has numerous short stories published in five anthologies and has written ten novels published on Amazon. Jon is a Marine.

Daneen Pysz
The story of Mary

Daneen has written many songs and stories about women in the Bible. She portrays and tells us these women's stories in a unique style. Her body of work is called, "The Bible's 'Bad' Girls".

The word bad can have a double meaning. For instance, in 1960's slang; if someone said, "Oh, that's bad!" they could have meant "Oh, that's good!" Daneen uses the double meaning of the word bad as she tells her stories about these amazing women who did brave and courageous deeds, and always for the glory and honor of God.

She is a member of Networking of Biblical Storytellers International, Marnie's Christian Women's Speaker Organization, Village Publishing Club, and a published author of two books.

Her books, *Bible's 'Bad' Girls...the lesser known brave and courageous women of the Bible* and *Royalty and Loyalty* can be purchased on Amazon.

S. Ramagopal
Big Bang
Bug
Korean Delight
Panoptic

Ramagopal is a retired scientist. He was educated and trained at the University of Madras, University of California, and Harvard. His research advanced knowledge relevant to solving problems in agriculture and medicine. He writes in English and Tamil, and has published three poetry collections. At present he is weathering his eleventh US President.

Daya Shankar-Fischer
The Old Red Brick Building: Lal Hebeli

Daya Shankar-Fischer a native of India lives in Laguna Hills, CA. Prior to this for few years she lived in Laguna Woods Village. After that she and her husband, Robert Fischer lived in Mission Viejo, CA. After her husband died, she moved to the Wellington (a long-term facility) in Laguna Hills, CA.

Daya was a professor at University of Northern Iowa. She earned her graduate degrees MA and Ph.D. in Philosophy and Communication from Ohio University, Athens Ohio. Her teaching profession offered her the opportunity to travel. She travelled to several countries. Some of her favorite ones include Italy, Ireland, England, Switzerland, England, Norway, Costa Rica, Spain, El Salvedore, Mexico, Thailand, and Malaysia. She retired as Professor Emeritus in 2001.

Daya keeps herself busy in reading, writing, and doing the humanitarian work. She supports the Native

American Education Foundations. Through this program the students in need receive scholarships.

Cheryl Silverman
Orange County
Palm
Senior Text-Back Symbols w/Phil Silverman
Tiny Gray Lizards

Cheryl Silverman is a 2011 California arrival by way of Michigan and Vegas, navigating a '08 Saturn Aura. Having retired from her position as Auto and Home Insurance Underwriter, she landed upon Caregiving Services.

Sidelight hobbies quickly became Quiddler, Puzzles, and Scrabble. Scrabble led to Haikus. Haikus led to the Publishing-Club.

See her work in the new Annual!

Phil Silverman
Another Fantasy Encounter with Abbott & Costello, Childhood Run, Foolish Me, I Need Me So, I Wonder Why I Wonder Why, Scenes from a Clubhouse, Senior Text-Back Symbols w/Cheryl Silverman, Sex & Violins, She Can Hardly Get Around, Strange as it Seems

Phil Silverman is somewhat of a Renaissance Man. Or as the humble Silverman will say, he simply is a creative multi-tasker.

He's from the Garden State, more specifically, the Jersey Shore, and he's bursting with memoirs of his many years as resident thereof.

Here he contributes sketches, poems, and Haikus (with his talented wife, Cheryl).

Phil has published six books as a member of the Club: *The Boomer Rang, The Boomer Rang Twice* (co-written by his wife, Cheryl Silverman), *The Totally Disappointing Seinfeld Reunion, The Boomer's Back!, The Boomer Sings Again!*, and *The Uncollected Boomer.*

He's proud to say he had a hand in building this vaunted Club; and that he's a participant in another Annual.

Peg Zuber
Everything I Need to Know I learned
*   From 12 Bible Stories*
When to Talk

Peg is a lifelong Californian, a graduate of Cal Poly, San Luis Obispo. For half of her 30-year career, she taught secondary level math in various districts from Camarillo to Capistrano; during the other half she was a software engineer for Teledyne and Litton. She has been married 56 years; raised three children; has a 17-year-old grandson and a 14-year-old cat. She has also written materials, organized, and taught Women's Bible Study groups through the years.

Since moving to Laguna Woods Village in 2000, she has participated in bridge, art, and church activities. During the COVID shutdown she resurrected and published an e-book she had started in 1994 while living in Camarillo, *-All I'll Ever Need to Know I Learned in Sunday School*; available now on Amazon. Being a member of the Publishing Club has reopened many areas of interest.

Afterword

Like so many groups, the Publishing Club learned to survive during the pandemic by initiating monthly Zoom Meetings for its members. Here's a picture from one of our Publishing Club's Zoom Meetings.

Spring in Laguna Woods
Sunshine Lutey

Sunset in Laguna Woods
Nancy Brown

Made in the USA
Las Vegas, NV
03 October 2021

31624066R00148